# Requiem for Torchy

Sarah,

I wrote this book for my sister who loved my brother Joe very much.

Tony

# Requiem for Torchy

◆

## The Life of a Gambler

*Tony Tripodi*

Writers Club Press

New York  Lincoln  Shanghai

# Requiem for Torchy
## The Life of a Gambler

Writers Club Press
an imprint of iUniverse, Inc.

For information address:
iUniverse, Inc.
2021 Pine Lake Road, Suite 100
Lincoln, NE 68512
www.iuniverse.com

ISBN: 0-595-26448-4

Printed in the United States of America

# *Contents*

# *Acknowledgements*

I thank my wife Miriam for encouraging me to write this book; my sister Phil and brother-in-law Aubrey, and Janice and Mary, Joe Torchia's ex-wives, who were gracious in providing me with information about my brother; countless other family members and friends who contributed to preserving Joe's memory; and Ronda Griffith-Grubb, who typed the manuscript.

# Introduction

This is a story about a gambler who lived in Sacramento, California. His name is Joe Torchia. It was 33 years ago that he was viciously murdered in his own home. The murder remains unsolved; yet the legend of Joe Torchia ("Torchy") and his extraordinary feats lived for many years after his death. Stories about him were told in bars, card rooms, horse races, and newspapers. He was regarded as one of the top three gamblers in Sacramento's history.

Joe is my brother. He was a charismatic character, a son of Italian immigrants. A complex person with a mixture of fears and hopes, Joe lived hard and died hard. I write about him now to celebrate his memory. His story is presented in vignettes that describe cross-sections of his life and times. These themes are covered: *Murder:* the Murder, the Funeral, Requiem, Mystery; *Youth:* Joe, the Sailboat, the Merchant Marine, the Bowling Alley, the Bakery; *Family:* Mother, Siblings, Wives, Children; *Gambling:* Crap Games, Poker, Lake Tahoe, Horse Races, the Downside of Bookmaking, The Buggy Whip; *Retirement Dreams:* Retirement, Resting; *Epilogue.*

# *Murder*

# THE MURDER

This column appeared in the *Sacramento Bee*, January 19, 1970, the day after my brother Joe was murdered.

## *"Restaurateur J.J. Torchia Is Murdered"*

"Joseph J. Joe Torchia, 41, operator of a Fulton Avenue restaurant, was shot to death in his Rancho Cordova home in a slaying which may involve a large amount of money."

"A brother and a friend discovered him dead in the bathroom of his home at 9401 Folsom Boulevard about 8:30 p.m. yesterday. He had been shot once in the shoulder and three times in the head."

"The coroner's deputies said he had been dead about two hours."

"Torchia was well known in horse race and bookmaking circles. He was arrested in July 1956 and again in March 1957 on bookmaking charges and both times the charges were dismissed before he went to trial."

"Torchia was known to carry large sums of money and some persons believe he may have had money hidden at his home. He had a reputation of 'flashing' large amounts in public places. An investigator stated Torchia was robbed and that a large amount of money is missing."

"Recently he had an interest in The Buggy Whip, a restaurant at 2737 Fulton Avenue."

"Sheriff's officers reported the bullets were fired through a pillow, apparently to muffle the sound of the shots."

"He is believed to have put up a fight and more than one person probably was involved. A well-built five feet 11, 206-pounder, Torchia's friends said he 'could not be taken easily.'"

"The buttons on his sweater were ripped off and his hands and legs were cut and bruised. Both eyes also were bruised black, but the coroner's deputies do not know if these were from a beating or from the gunshots."

"Deputies are investigating a possibility he may have been beaten before he was killed in an effort to force him to disclose money he may have had hidden."

"His wife, Jeanne, is reported by the officers to have taken a trip to Stateline yesterday. She was contacted late last night."

Joe Torchia is my half-brother. We had the same mother but different fathers. I loved Joe as a brother, whole heartedly. At the time of his murder I was a professor of research in the School of Social Work, University of Michigan, Ann Arbor, Michigan. I hadn't seen him since I left California in 1966; but I continued to love and respect him, and thought of him as my "big brother," who was my protector throughout childhood. When the phone rang late at night Sunday, January 18, 1970, I was alarmed. I usually did not receive calls in the middle of the night. My half-sister Phil told me Joe was murdered, and when and where the funeral would be held. After I hung up, I simply cried, again and again.

My pain was shared by all of those who knew him, especially by my sister Phil and my half-brother Tommy who were his siblings and had been close to him all their lives. Whereas Joe was my big brother, he was Tommy and Phil's little brother. It was Tommy who found Joe dead in his bathroom. He was horrified to see blood splattered all over the bathroom, the mirrors, the walls, the floor; and he was shocked and shaking over the sight of his beloved brother, grotesquely disfigured as a result of fighting and gunshots.

Phil said that she was playing Bingo the night of the murder and felt something was wrong before she received the news. She had a premonition of pain. She had a severe headache and tears came to her eyes. People who played near her gave her aspirin and water. When she heard of Joe's death, she too cried. She was angry at everyone who had hurt him throughout his life and was ready to take revenge on whoever it was that killed him.

Joe died suddenly at a relatively young age, forty-one. His death made me think of past deaths of loved ones, my mother and father, as well as several quick snapshots of my life with him, especially as a young boy. Both of my parents' deaths were gradual. My father died of leukemia and was severely sick several years before his death. My mother died of advanced symptoms of diabetes, having progressed over four years before her death to blindness and gangrene.

I thought of Joe's life as a gambler and the many risks he took. I wondered whether or not his murder was planned by those with whom he came into contact, or by those who had insurance policies on his life, or even by the nebulous Mafia. My wife at the time, was three weeks' pregnant with my son David, and I wondered whether David's new life would have any of the characteristics of Joe's old life.

My family was relatively poor when I was a child. Joe gave me money for doing odd jobs for him, like washing the car, helping him sell cushions at midget auto races, cleaning the house, and so forth. He ultimately warned me about gambling, not to do it; yet, he took me to poker games and crap games to teach me something about them. Perhaps, that's why I became interested in statistics and probability, which I taught at various universities. Although Joe was a high school drop-out, he was certainly a practitioner of statistics and probability. A knowledge of chance and "odds" was basic to his practice as a book-maker and as a gambler. The odds were not in his favor in the game of life Sunday, January 18, 1970.

He exuded life and sparked an eager interest in simple pleasures, recreation, eating, and family relationships. Joe's life was full of episodes—funny, tragic, and heart rending. My sister thought of a time when he was young and was apparently drowning in the American River. A neighbor, a young boy, saved his life. Joe hit him because he thought the boy was trying to drown him. That boy became a friend. In adulthood, Joe lent him money to help him in his business activities. He paid Joe off a few days before Joe's death.

Joe's murder was violent and brutal. His life was cut short, and his friends and relatives were in a state of shock. We were in the epicenter of an earthquake and would find ourselves feeling aftershocks of the tragedy as more information would be revealed. But death has no compassion for the living. As in poker, we must cope with the cards that are dealt us. To this day thirty-three years after his murder, which was never solved, the aftershocks of his death persist.

# THE FUNERAL

I flew from Detroit, Michigan, to Sacramento, California, January 20, 1970. For the most part, I felt numb on the flight. My thoughts were pervaded by sadness, anxiety, and apprehension about the funeral. It was a time for reflection. I thought of a funeral as a place for friends and relatives to gather, exchanging words about the person being honored. At funerals we talk about the person's contributions to her or his family, as well as the nature of the death; and words like this came to mind: "He died too young." "He gave so much to his family." "I hope they find the murderer." "What a tragedy." "Why does this happen to our family?" "Look at all the people who came to pay their respects." "He was a good man." "We will always remember him."

Thoughts in anticipation of the funeral led me to reflect on the funerals of my mother, my father, and my brother Joe's father. My mother was sixty-two when she died of pneumonia, having suffered from advanced stages of sugar diabetes the previous four years. She was blind and had a foot amputated due to gangrene. In her last hours, not even the morphine could ease the pain. My mother's death was perceived as a relief, for her as well as for my sister who took care of her. We didn't want my mother to die because we didn't want to lose her presence, the evidence of her spirit in our worlds. She was entombed in St. Mary's Mausoleum in Sacramento. The funeral was one of sadness but one which had been expected. Nothing but simple love was expressed and the fact that she worked hard to better the conditions of her children.

My father's funeral was the first one I could remember. He was a young man, thirty-six, who died of leukemia in a hospital in San Francisco. He was buried in the poor section of St. Mary's Cemetery since my mother could not afford anything else. We were, in fact, poor. My mother's entombment in a wall of St. Mary's Mausoleum eighteen years later reflected upward mobility in the cemetery as well as in the life she provided for her family. One year earlier, November, 1940, I traveled with my brother Joe, sister Phil and my mother to Ithaca, New York, to attend the funeral of Joe's father. I don't remember attending the funeral, but I do recall certain events that took place. My brother Joe taught me how to tell time on the train to New York. In Ithaca we had contests like these: determining who could drink the most glasses of water laced with salt and pepper; and seeing who could keep an item of food the longest without eating it, thereby taunting the other one for not having any food. Although I had never seen Joe's father, I heard that he was a happy-go-lucky man who drank a lot and sang a lot. In fact, it was his drunkenness that led my mother to divorce him in 1932. Ironically, Joe appeared to have inherited many of his characteristics. Like his father, Joe drank and gambled frequently. Even as an adolescent Joe set pins in a bowling alley in Sacramento just like his father did in Ithaca, New York. Sometimes, Joe's father was so drunk that he couldn't work at the gun factory in Ithaca. My mother had to replace him at work so that he could keep his job. An event in Joe's life was similar to one in his father's life. Both of them drank and smoked. They both had the same experience of smoking in bed, falling asleep, and waking up to a fire. Neither one was injured.

When I arrived in Sacramento to attend the funeral, this item appeared in the *Sacramento Bee*, January 20, 1970:

## *"Murder Probe Bares $7,000 Robbery of Victim"*

"Sheriff's detectives today conducted interviews and sifted evidence in a search for clues leading to the killers of Joseph J. 'Torchy' Torchia, 41, restaurant manager and horse race figure who was robbed and shot to death Sunday in his home at 9401 Folsom Boulevard."

"The investigators said he was robbed of approximately $7,000, part of which was money he was carrying for The Buggy Whip, a restaurant at 2737 Fulton Avenue, and part of which was his own money."

"Torchia was known by many persons to carry large sums of money."

"Reports indicated he also had a large amount of cash hidden in his home, but friends close to him doubted he had a big cache recently because the race tracks in California have been closed by a strike."

"He last was seen alive when he left The Buggy Whip about 7:30 p.m. Sunday. Two friends apparently just missed happening upon his slaying. They arrived at his home in Rancho Cordova at 7:55 p.m. After a few minutes delay when he failed to answer the doorbell they entered the house and discovered him dead in the bathroom."

"It would have taken 10 to 15 minutes for him to reach his residence from the restaurant."

"Put Up Battle"

"More than one person is believed to have been waiting for him. Probably someone who knew him. A rugged 200-pounder who had a reputation of being without fear of any man, Torchia apparently put up a battle."

"One bullet went through his right shoulder, causing him to bleed profusely. He then was shot two or three times in his head in the bathroom off the master bedroom."

"His wife, Jeanne, had gone to Stateline."

"In addition to her, he is survived by his children, Joseph and Maria Torchia and Susan and Michael Campanella; a brother, Thomas, and a sister, Philomena Halsted all of Sacramento, and another brother, Dr. Tony Tripodi of Ann Arbor, Michigan."

"A rosary will be said tomorrow night in the Lombard & Co. Funeral Home. Services will be held at 9:00 a.m. Thursday in the funeral home and a mass will be offered at 10 a.m. Thursday in St. Mary's Church. Entombment will be in St. Mary's Mausoleum."

Joe's casket was closed throughout the services and the funeral. His body was apparently too disfigured to show. This made me feel angry at the murderer, for I couldn't see Joe one more time before his entombment. He had many friends and acquaintances. Many were governmental employees and the police; others were lawyers, doctors, and businessmen; still others were clients and associates in his gambling and restaurant endeavors. Rumor had it that many people didn't come to the funeral because they didn't want to be implicated in the murder. There appears to have been a ring of truth to this. Even recently when I requested information about his life from his friends, I received no assistance. Perhaps, people wanted to leave stories about him in the past. Perhaps, there was a fear that I was trying to solve his murder. Perhaps, there was a persisting fear of being implicated in some way.

The funeral was strange. It had the feeling of a Mafia movie, that it was unreal. Joe's wife and children were there, as well as the families of my sister and my brother Tommy. There was an underlying anxiety that the murderer might be attending the funeral. There was shock, sadness and anger, all mingled in gloomy clouds of fear. Was someone out to get his family as well? Was the murderer a close friend or relative? I found myself conjecturing as to who the murderer might be. However, I knew that I was not interested in revenge. My brother was gone, and nothing could restore him in my eyes.

We were in Joe's house. The bathroom where he was found had been cleaned. Friends and relatives were crying and reminiscing. His wife Jeanne and some others began to discuss his will and what would become of the property he owned. My sister was grieving over his death and didn't want to discuss money one hour after his entombment. The discussion went on in complete oblivion of Joe's death. The voices became a constant din surrounding my weeping sister. It was rumored that his wife Jeanne had taken out a $100,000 life insurance policy on Joe six months before his death. Although she was in Stateline, gambling in Nevada where it was legal, the night of his murder, there was speculation that she might have been involved in the crime. That hypothesis has never been substantiated, but it was entertained, rightly or wrongly, by some members of Joe's family.

The reception after the funeral was a demonstration of our human frailties. Some simply grieved. Others were thinking seriously about their future. Still others were perplexed. Emotions and frustrations emerged, and there was the underlying expression of love and remembrance, with a premature finality in the sealing of Joe's tomb.

# REQUIEM

"Requiem": It means "rest," and it denotes a mass for the dead.[1] The requiem is based on music, prose, and poetry; and it is intended to be inspirational and awe-inspiring. The words and music of a requiem preserve the memory of the dead.

My brother's death is the final event of his life. A mass for the dead was given in his name to honor his life. He is also honored by the words we read, speak, and write about him. This book is an accounting of some major events in his life and death. It is, so to speak, a requiem.

My brother Joe had four different newspaper articles written about him over a span of eighteen years since his death. They provide words about a character of Damon Runyan-like qualities, a requiem to him and a remembrance of a gambler. The first article was published January 20, 1970, in *The Sacramento Union*, a morning newspaper, two days after his death. It was written by an outstanding sports columnist:

## *"Torchy Involved in First Crime"*
### *by Bill Conlin*
### *Sacramento Union Sports Editor*

"Joe Torchia, whose murder Sunday night shocked the Sacramento Community, was an inveterate gambler and completely honest."

"Years ago, a wagering friend known as the Philosopher argued late into the night that there was no such thing as an honest professional gambler."

"'The breed,' he said, 'simply does not exist.'"

"'How about Torchy?' someone asked."

"The Philosopher stood on his head in a Yoga position and meditated for minutes. Finally he reversed his perpendicularity and agreed: 'I can't think of another one. Torchy is the exception that proves the rule.'"

---

1.    Webster's Ninth New College Dictionary, Merriam-Webster, Inc., Publishers, Springfield, Massachusetts, U.S.A., 1990, p. 1002.

"Torchy had absolutely no enemies and thousands of friends, which makes his demise the more distressing."

"His good works were hidden in anonymity, but he was a soft touch for the dolorous story. In short, he made money but he spread it, too."

"Torchia was in business many years, but there never came to light a story about a person he cheated."

"In matters of controversy, he leaned over backward. His was the old time bookmakers' theory: 'In order to have losers, you must have winners. Everybody should win occasionally, but not too often.'"

### "Really Takes the Cake"

"For more than half his life, Torchy was a gambler. But if he had to list an occupation he probably would have called himself a cake decorator."

"That was his first job, but he didn't stick with it long."

"At the end of the first week during which he worked 60 hours and ran up a lot of overtime, the young fellow went to his boss at the old Channel Pie Co."

"'I'll tell you what,' he proposed. 'For the week's pay I'll shake you double or nothing.' It was the end of a career."

"About this time, after he had mastered cake decorating, Torchy learned Pinochle. This caused a turnaround in his career."

"The pastry world was the loser, but the gambling world was enhanced by a square gee who gave the sucker a chance."

"Torchy cut his eyeteeth in an old Sunday morning crap game that used to operate at a local produce market. He was a kid of 17 or 18 but he brought burly truck drivers to their knees in literal and figurative sense."

### "Unusual Horse Sense"

"Theologians might disagree, but to the young kid the logic was irrefutable: 'Why work six days a week,' he said, 'when all this loot is available on the seventh?'"

"Torchy was only 41 when he came to his end, and he was in no sense an intellectual. Fact is, he might have been a school dropout."

"But he had a mathematical mind that directed into more useful pursuits would have intrigued Einstein."

"Horse players ranked him ne plus ultra as a 'figures man.' He could subtract more out of the Racing form than a half dozen ordinary players in tandem."

"Odds and betting prices were his meat and potatoes. He could look at a form and check it with the tote board and reach conclusions that are deprived the ordinary mortal."

"Yet, as well as we knew Torchy, and the friendship covered many years, he never volunteered a tip. He kept his own counsel on the subject he knew best, which was horses."

"He once explained it this way: 'I'll talk to you about the stock market, or baseball, or even football. These are subjects I only know casually. But horses I've been too close to, and people expect too much if I give them a tip. There are 1,000 ways to lose a horse race, and exactly that many ways to lose a friend. I keep my mouth shut around the track when I'm with friends.'"

"Joe Torchia was a Sacramento institution, and a great fellow. There are a tremendous number of persons disconsolate in his death."

Two days later, January 22, 1970, another exceptional sports writer, Marco Smolich, wrote about my brother Joe. In his column he recognized and reported on unusual events that emerged into the character called Torchy:

"Sitting alone at the bar was a well-dressed, middle-aged man who had just finished his first Scotch-and-soda and ordered a second. After being served the drink, he moved the ice around with a finger, meditatively, and kept talking to the bartender. 'Yeah, they buried Joe Torchia today.' Restaurateur, gambler—call him what you want, but with him probably went the last of Sacramento's big spenders. I mean guys who aren't looking for publicity, who just want to do what they think is right. In a way, an introvert. What Damon Runyan couldn't have done with Joe Torchia."

"Honest and generous, a guy who believed deep down in moral obligations. He'd spend 50 bucks on you—but if you owed him a dime for three weeks, he'd remember it. That, to Torchy, was an obligation, however small. And don't think for a moment that Joe was always flush because I recall days he borrowed from close friends to pay debts."

"Torchy was only 15 when he enlisted in the Merchant Marine during World War II. Even then gambling was life to him—and he brought along cards and dice. Before his first ship returned home he had everybody in his pocket. What a gambler, what patience, what a memory. The stories about him you wouldn't believe."

"I'm at the Elks Lodge several years ago and Torchy shows up for the amateur fights. There's a can on the bar and all the money goes for the cerebral palsy fund. After a while Joe asks the bartender, 'How much is in here?' and the bartender answers, 'About $200.' So the Torch peels off bills, tosses them into the can—matching the $200. Then he walks away, like nothing happened."

"I'm not going to mention how good he was to his own kids, his family. Everybody knows. But there was this one kid, about 16, whose dad dies. The family has no dough. Lives in Joe's neighborhood but he doesn't even know their name. Still, when he hears what happened, he goes to them, insists on leaving money and gets the boy a job in a restaurant."

"Torchy had to be the greatest coin lagger and tosser in the world. At Sac High he'd break the frat boys. He had a fantastic determination to win, at anything, pool, cards, horses. Anything."

"We're at Santa Rosa, and, after the races, Joe wants to throw coins for prizes. Almost every time he throws, he wins. Finally the guy in the booth says, 'You've had it, partner. You're too good.' We needed two boxes to cart the stuff away. The Torch goes to another booth and asks, 'What's the limit here?' He's told, 'As long as you keep tossing dimes, you can take home the joint.' Well, he wins two more box loads with a big crowd watching before he quits."

"On the way out a cute little girl talks to him, looking at those prizes with big eyes, and she's joined by two sisters and her mother. You can tell they're poor. What does Joe do? Just gives them all four boxes—and tells me, 'Hell, they'd have been busted up before we got to Sacramento. You're a lousy driver. Never miss a bump.'"

"Another time at Vallejo he talks a friend into betting $20 a throw on shooting basketballs through hoops. Torchy loses the first throw—and they keep it up until he blows $200. Joe knew this guy had problems, that he needed money—and that was his way of giving it to him."

"You think he lost all that weight, from 260 to 199, on doctor's advice? Nonsense. He did it to win a $100 bet. And, listen, this was a tough person with absolutely no fear. He had his share of alley fights and when he lost he'd just laugh—even with a broken nose and bloody face."

"Thieves would seek him at the track and he'd listen to all, politely, but not caring. Sometimes he'd hide to keep away from guys who'd gone Tap City. Once they got to him, he couldn't refuse."

"One day at the State Fair meeting he blows $4,800. He's mad and says, 'I'm getting out of here.' I see him the next day and he tells me, 'I went up to the Lake and won $4,900.' I say, 'Great, Torchy, so you didn't get hurt.' He says, 'Didn't get hurt? Hell, if I hadn't dropped the $4,800 I'd be $4,900 ahead.'"

"Call him gambler or whatever you want. But here, friend, was a man."

Fifteen years later, December 9, 1985, another article appeared in the *Sacramento Bee*, the evening newspaper. This article described Sacramento's "golden era of gambling," featuring three gamblers, including my brother Joe. Bob Sylva puts the memory of Joe Torchia in the context of historic gambling in the capital city of California.

## *"A Few Colorful Characters Enliven Capital Gambling's Famed Past"*
*Bob Sylva*
*Bee Staff Writer*

"The biggest gamble hereabouts happened in 1849, when thousands of hopefuls took a flier on a long shot called gold. Alas, most of those players lapped out."

"In considering the more organized games of chance that followed, not much has changed."

"Since Sacramento's earliest incarnation as a tent city overrun with hordes of rapscallions, card sharps and flimflam artists to its august status now as a seat of state government, wagering has been a shadowy fact of the city's life, but most of it is and has been at the nickel and dime level."

"From office pools to football cards, faro tables to low ball rooms, dance saloons to charity sponsored 'casino nights' gambling-both legal and illegal—has manifested itself in a variety of forms, in a range of venues."

"Despite the pervasiveness of the pasttime, none of it has been sorely blatant and there are few, if any, indications that it has been inordinately profitable, or more romantic yet, controlled by the 'mob.' Big spenders in Sacramento have traditionally preferred to risk their bankroll in real estate, where pulse-quickening deals and jackpot payoffs make most forms of odds-play superfluous."

"Not that Sacramento has been bereft of action and some picaresque players. Long before Old Sacramento was a scrubbed hub for souvenir T-shirts and simulated train whistles, it was a full-blown and seedily authentic skid row, boasting flop houses, soup kitchens and a few early versions of singles' bars. It was a spot where a sporting man could toss back a shot and lay a wager."

"It was here in the city's West End that gambling first took root, flourished and branched out. It was here, during the 1920's and early '30s that bookie joints operated openly, the constabulary palmed a weekly payoff and a few hardy entrepreneurs made the seed money for new legitimate family fortunes."

"According to many still living oldtimers, the most canny of the city's early wheeler-dealers was a dapper little man named Lazarus Bloomberg, a native of Edinburgh, Scotland, whose family immigrated to Sacramento in 1884."

"Bloomberg, who once worked as a boilermaker for Southern Pacific, later operated a cigar shop at 1021 2nd St. Again according to reliable sources (these things aren't exactly documented in the county recorder's office), at the rear of Bloomberg's shop was secreted a busy booking operation, where one could play the ponies at tracks across the country."

"Bloomberg, jockey-size and a genial sort, was evidently a shrewd businessman. As his shop flourished, he turned his attention to an even more lucrative turf: downtown real estate."

"He ultimately became a prosperous respected civic leader, as well as a prominent figure in the city's Jewish community. On Bloomberg's and his wife's 50th wedding anniversary, no less a sport than President John F. Kennedy made a call of congratulations. Not a bad deal."

"Taking over the odds' chalkboard abdicated by Bloomberg was another European immigrant—Frank J. 'Butch' Nisetich, an ox-like, affable man, who came to Sacramento from the Yugoslavian island of Brac. He was arguably the most celebrated gambler in the city's history. Unlike Bloomberg, Nisetich, once flush, remained a betting man his entire life."

"Nicknamed 'Butch' for his short stint as a butcher, Nisetich raised his original stake during World War I. Along with enduring the dangers of the Argonne forest as a U.S. soldier, he managed to survive many a perilous hand of poker. One story has it that he regularly sent home envelopes filled with his winnings."

"It was this cash that Nisetich used to bankroll his first enterprise—the Equipoise cardroom and bar at 415 K St. Even the start of that fabled Sacramento club deserves a small footnote."

"According to a knowledgeable source Nisetich once went to see Laz Bloomberg to make a sporting proposition. Incensed at the tight odds that the old man was offering, Nisetich was approached by an enterprising police captain who, proffering patronage of sorts, said in effect, 'This town is big enough for two bookmakers.' Thus, Butch was in business."

"The Equipoise became Sacramento's premier cardroom and horse-betting parlor. Gamblers from across the country would try their luck against 'Sacramento Butch' in card games that went on for days, while thoroughbred enthusiasts, like celebrated lobbyist Artie Samish—who legend has it, habitually bet $1,000 a race—populated the upstairs horse book. The Equipoise, with a nice bar and restaurant, was a going concern."

"Though Nisetich was twice charged and tried for bookmaking, he was never convicted. He finally closed the Equipoise horse book in 1936 (the cardroom was apparently more profitable anyway), and pursued other interests in town. One hobby of his was bowling at which he similarly excelled. Cool and unflappable, Butch took on all comers and covered all bets. Surrounded by loyal cronies, his was the classic sporting life."

"Nisetich retired in comfort to Aptos around 1950. His beach house reportedly had two telephones. Moving from cards and horses, he gambled in the stock market. And he continued to best the odds. He died in 1975, at 89, a wealthy and much admired man."

"The last personality to close out what might be considered Sacramento's golden era of gambling was Joe Torchia. Tall, dark, appealing to the ladies and handy with his fists, Torchia—nick-named 'Torchy'—fit the popular image of the nattily dressed, good-looking, somewhat glamorous gambler."

"A local boy, Torchia was into action as early as high school, where he reportedly lagged for quarters at Sacramento High. Later he enlisted in the Merchant Marine as a teenager, and further polished his card-playing skills. Driven by a keen desire to compete, Torchia would reputedly bet on anything—from dice or cards to the dime toss at the county fair."

"Arrested twice on bookmaking charges in the late '50s, Torchia beat both raps. He later owned a piece of The Buggy Whip restaurant out on Fulton Avenue, and according to friends familiar with the atmosphere, Torchia continued to bankroll a bookmaking operation that did a nice handle on horses."

"'Joe was a master of the collect,' says one small-time bookie in Sacramento. 'He knew just when to show up to get his money. He had a sense. He was something else.' Others recall Torchia's integrity, generosity, and his unfailing memory to recall an outstanding debt. Such traits stood him well in his fast-track lifestyle."

"But Torchia's luck ran out on the night of January 18, 1970. Returning home from the restaurant, Torchia was killed by waiting assailant(s), who shot the gambler three times in the head. Torchia, game to the end, didn't go down without a fight. His battered body was discovered in the bathroom of his Rancho Cordova home. He was 41 years old."

"Police then theorized robbery was a motive, and reported $7,000 missing from Torchia's person. But over the years, Torchia assassination scenarios have become popular barroom guessing games. 'We have a pretty good idea who did it,' says one veteran police lieutenant today. 'But we'll never be able to prove it.' 'The suspected killer,' says this officer, 'continues to live and gamble in Sacramento…'"

The last article serving as a requiem to my brother Joe eighteen years after his death, was also written by Bob Sylva of the *Sacramento Bee*, January 17, 1988, in the *Sacramento Bee Magazine*. It not only pays tribute to his memory, but it also raises a question about his murder.

## *"Remembering Torchy"*

"…It's a recent weekday morning at a downtown bar. Outside a pale sky is chafed by a bitter wind. Inside, a huddle of old men are drinking coffee laced with brandy and grousing about life and sports, for the most part. With the Super Bowl imminent, the wagering season reaches its frantic apogee."

"Buzz Jones is sitting at a side table smoking a cigarette. Jones isn't his real name. Jones requests anonymity since he's been known to place a bet here and there, and there's little to gain in advertising the fact. Jones is a gambler, has been his whole life. And as a player, he knew Joe Torchy. 'He was my best friend,' says Jones loyally. For old time's sake, he recalls his pal with a measure of pride and sad longing."

"Joe grew up around C Street. He was a tough kid, scrappy and streetwise. At Sacramento High School, he earned pocket money lagging for coins. When there was cash on the line, nobody could beat Joe. At anything. As a young kid, he worked as a pinsetter at the old Alhambra Bowl, where he became friends with Butch Nisetich, then the reigning oddsman in Sacramento. Butch took Torchy under his wing and treated him like a son. After a stint in the Merchant Marine—where he perfected his poker game—Torchy came home and went into business for himself. He got involved peripherally in the state's profitable horse-racing industry. His office was a phone booth outside the old Trio Club on Broadway. And Joe, gifted equally with gall, a head for figures, and a streak of uncanny luck, did well."

"It was his personality as much as anything. 'Everybody liked Joe,' says Jones. 'He was so honest. His word was his bond. He never cheated anybody out of a dime.'"

"He had a shrewd if sympathetic business style. 'He would never resort to violence,' says Jones of money due. He would just say, 'Just make it easy on yourself. Just give me a date when you can pay it off. But you'd better be true to your word.'"

"But more than a gambler, Joe was a character. Impulsive, he would fly down to Hollywood Park on a moment's notice if a horse he liked was running that day. Charismatic, he'd walk into a bar, throw a wad of bills down and grandly set the place up. Reckless, Joe would bet on anything—anything. Though he didn't golf, he would settle old scores on the putting green at Land Park and invariably win. At the State Fair, when he wasn't playing the horses, he'd pitch dimes until he was banned from the midway. Afterward, he'd give away all the stuffed animals like a Santa Claus. Joe had a soft spot for kids, and his philanthropies were legion. He was gruff, boisterous, at times obnoxious, but still much beloved."

"So why was he murdered? 'I think they (thieves) thought it was going to be a simple robbery,' surmises Jones. 'And Joe put up a flight. Everybody knew he carried big sums of money.' Others draw a more chilling scenario, that Joe was hit by some syndicate wise guys usurping his turf. It's even widely rumored that the police know the identity of his killer(s) but lack sufficient evidence for an arrest. In any event, the legend of Joe Torchy lives on…"

Joe's requiem is not one that rests in peace, with Gregorian chants singing to the dead. He is remembered, and people speak of him and his feats as Torchy, the legend. In Sacramento, he was a gambling icon. But beneath words of praise and the recalling of his extraordinary antics there lurks an underlying tension about his unsolved murder. Why was he murdered? Did more than one person murder him? Did the police really suspect who was involved, without interrogating him, her, or them? Was it connected to the Mafia, or was it murder for hire?

# MYSTERY

The headline in the *Sacramento Union*, three days after his murder, exclaimed, "Torchia Murder Still a Mystery." Apparently, along with my brother Joe, the investigation had been laid to rest. There was a flurry of police and newspaper activity for approximately two to three months. It began with a bang and died out in a whimper as a bizarre series of events occurred.

Shortly after Joe's death, the *Sacramento Union* (January 20, 1970) reported:

> "Authorities believe more than one person was waiting for Torchia on his arrival."
>
> "Sheriff's officers said a struggle ensued inside the house. There were bullet markings in the walls of the home's master bedrooms and 'marks' and scratches along the hallway. Both of the victim's eyes were blackened, there were cuts and bruises on his hands and legs, and buttons from his sweater had been torn off."
>
> "Sources theorized that Torchia was beaten by his attackers in hopes the victim would lead them to a hiding place where money was stashed. They said Torchia might have tried to get a revolver he reportedly kept in the mattress of his bed."
>
> "The murder weapon was not found. The slugs reportedly were fired from a .38-caliber weapon, sources said..."

The following report in the *Sacramento Union*, January 22, 1970, describes some theories about the murder, provides some possible clues, indicates a large amount of police activity, and ends with the prophecy that the Joe Torchy murder will not be solved:

# "Torchia Investigators Batting Zero"
### by Steve Pence
### Sacramento Union Staff Writer

"Five days after the murder of Sacramento's No. 1 gambler, Joseph 'Joe Torchy' Torchia, it appears sheriff's detectives have reached an impasse."

"Authorities have maintained the customary official silence about details of the investigation."

"But the circumstances of Joe Torchy's violent, chilling murder have prompted widespread reports in private circles that he was the victim of more than just a robbery that turned into a killing."

"One thing is certain: Joe Torchy had friends everywhere. He spent almost all his life in this area and over the years the heavyset gambler accumulated a long line of friends who described him this past week as the sort of character with a big heart and—if needed—a heavy hand."

"An insight to Torchy's non-gangster demeanor was best related by a longtime friend. On the way to a Bay area race track, Torchy once sidetracked his traveling companions—who were eager to be on time for the Daily Double—at the Nut Tree gift shop off Interstate 80. He had to stop, he said, to buy a special toy for one of his children."

"They still laugh fondly at the Joe Torchy who would bet in five figures but wince at paying a $1.50 entry fee into the race grandstand. At one race track, he relished a secret entryway—a break in the surrounding gate—and was wont to leave his friends and enter through it. On one occasion, friends say, his trousers snagged and were ripped out spilling a bankroll estimated in the thousands of dollars."

"It's no secret that Torchy counted as close friends a number of men who happened to work as policemen. A few of those friends are now working on their own time in hope of finding the killer, or killers."

"And so friends who know and bet with him ask out loud, 'Why would anyone want to kill Torchy?' Some discount robbery for a simple reason: He had been robbed at least six times, none of which was reported to authorities. Knowing that Torchy carried large sums of money on his person and in his car, a thief once stole the expensive automobile, extracted some money, then gratefully called Torchy and told him where the car was parked."

"…Authorities disclosed only that Torchy had been slain by intruders. They said a struggle had taken place, that bullet marks were found in the walls of the master bedroom, that 'marks' were found in the hallway (indicating a struggle) and the killers apparently escaped with some money."

"Another report, that a pair of bloodied ladies gloves were found in the yard, has been discounted. Officers also found two pistols belonging to Torchy inside the house."

"Did the killers intercept Torchy, or were they waiting inside the house? Authorities have declined comment."

"The only neighbors within earshot are believed to be a woman identified as Torchy's mother-in-law and her practical nurse. The reason they heard nothing that night can be attributed to a 'professional' technique used by the killers: Pillows were wrapped around the murder weapon."

"Another foggy spot in the murder is the presence of two German Shepherd dogs who roam the acreage around the house. Although authorities had originally been informed that the dogs might be dangerous, they later proved gentle—perhaps docile—when first approached by investigating officers."

"Authorities have no reports of suspicious persons in the area on the night of the crime. It also has been learned that two suspects, one a Bay area man who reportedly had threatened Torchy, have been cleared."

"A few officials have expressed befuddlement over one aspect of the murder. Bullet holes were noted in the walls of the bedroom, but no blood was found in the room. The victim was shot in the back of the head, in the front near the eye, in the forehead and the shoulder."

"One source has commented that the slugs may be untraceable, keeping investigators from learning if more than one weapon was fired."

"A final question centers on the alleged hiding place for large sums of money, a trademark of gamblers. Sources believe Torchy had up to $100,000 concealed in the house, but that has been discounted by investigators."

"Although authorities appear to be at an impasse, a record number of detectives is attempting to solve the crime. Insiders, however, are predicting the Joe Torchy murder will go down as an 'unsolvable' crime."

In addition to police involvement, the *Sacramento Bee* in their secret witness program posted a reward of $2,500 which would have paid for information leading to the arrest and conviction of the killers.

The first major suspect was Leonard 'Babe' Bua, who was my godmother's son and a pall bearer at my brother Joe's funeral. He was a friend of the family and also worked as a maitre d' at The Buggy Whip, the restaurant in which Joe was a silent partner. Babe Bua, ex-football player and body builder, was arrested on a charge of conspiracy to commit armed robbery. However, he was subsequently released on the grounds of insufficient evidence. And then a young woman who was physically abused by her boyfriend reported him to the police saying that he was involved in the murder and that he worked for the Mafia. Authorities discounted Mafia involvement because there was no evidence of Mafia activity according to the Sheriff.

The woman's boyfriend, John R. Garcia, was a prime suspect one month after the murder. Garcia was with three women in an apartment in Reno, Nevada, when Sacramento sheriff's officers and Reno policemen arrested him. Arrest was not easy. There was a shootout. The officers knocked on the apartment door, identified themselves, and were greeted by gunfire. Garcia was finally subdued by tear gas; a detective was wounded, as well as one of the women who was shot in the stomach. Garcia was jailed in Reno, charged with attempted murder (of the policemen) and with conspiracy to commit robbery the night of Joe's murder. Two of the women were released, but another one was also charged as being an accomplice of Garcia. Another associate of Garcia's was also charged with conspiracy to commit armed robbery. The charges in Reno were dropped, and Garcia went to jail and court in Sacramento. All of the suspects of Joe's murder, including Garcia, were released since there was no evidence linking them to either robbery or the murder.

After all of the activity from hopeful newspaper reports to a shoot-out, alleged Mafia ties, and arrests, the prediction of an unsolved crime came true. No other leads appear to have been followed, and the investigation died down. It is very difficult to understand why a blatant, bloody murder was not able to be solved. Did the detectives have other suspects? Did family members have anything to do with the murder? Were there persons who collected huge benefits from insurance policies. And, if so, could they have played a part in the murder? There are many questions that were not answered. At one point, approximately a year after the murder, my sister and I contacted the police department seeking more information about the efforts of the police to solve the murder but this was to no avail. Did they know more than was released in the newspapers? Perhaps, the authorities really didn't want to solve the murder; or perhaps, it was a perfect crime, with no clues traceable to anyone. More than likely, we will never know. The mystery of his murder continues. Who did it, and why? What I do know is that Joe is dead, but his memory lives. Solving the murder cannot eradicate these basic facts. If the killer(s) were to be caught, my family might feel justifiable revenge is sweet. But it could only be bitter-sweet.

# *Youth*

# JOE

Joe Torchia was an Italian-American. He was not chauvinistically proud of his heritage, nor did he deny his Italian ancestry like some second and third generation Italians who do not want to be associated with the Mafia, thereby denouncing their Italian roots. Joe never discussed his Italian heritage nor the Mafia. But one knew he was unmistakably Italian, watching him wolf down a jar of pepperoncinis, a hunk of pepperoni, and a loaf of Italian bread, washing them down with cold beer or wine. Although he could have had some connection with the Mafia, I doubt it. Both our mother, Christina Grandinetti, and his father, Frank Torchia, were from Calabria, the foot of the boot of Italy, rather than from Sicily, the home of many Dons, fictional and otherwise. It was Willie the "Weasel," a Mafia informer who referred to Joe Torchia many years ago as a small-time, West Coast gambler who thought he was "hot stuff." He thought of Joe as a punk, not a made man as in Mafia folklore.

Frank Torchia, Joe's father, immigrated to America settling in Ithaca, New York, the home of Cornell University and the gun factory. The city was divided into the "gown" in the hills where a world-class university thrived and the "town" in the flats where many town people and immigrants worked at the gun factory. As was the custom, Italian immigrants, males, asked for prospective wives to be sent from Italy. It was arranged that Christina would emigrate from San Pietro d'Apostolo (St. Peter the Apostle), Calabria, to Ithaca, New York, to marry Frank Torchia. My mother had no idea of what her future husband would be like. She came by ship and was cooped up in small spaces with many other immigrants. Close quarters, sea sickness, and lice made for what might have been an unpleasant trip. Her eyes smiled one day when I asked her if she had ever loved anyone. She spoke of a time many years ago when she fell in love with a young man on the ship crossing the Atlantic. However, duty prevailed, and my mother continued her journey from Ellis Island to Ithaca without the young man. Frank and Christina married, settled, and had two children before Joe was conceived—Philomena (Phil) seven years older than Joe and Thomas (Tommy) one year younger than Phil.

Frank and Christina managed to acquire a boarding house and a chicken coop on Cascadilla Street. The day Joe was born Christina had gone to the chicken coop to kill chickens and cook them for the boarders. She had labor pains and went into the bedroom. A midwife delivered the baby. My sister Phil sat outside the bedroom window hearing my mother scream as if she were exploding. It was July 4, 1928, and the firecracker baby Joe Torchia was born. Frank Torchia was beside himself with joy carrying Joe around, while singing and staggering. He was drunk, regarded as happy-go-lucky on the surface, but was abusive and mean to his wife. Frank drank heavily, gambled, and worked in the gun factory. At times he got so drunk that my mother had to substitute for him at work so he would keep the job. Just as Joe would do when he was a teenager, Frank set pins in a bowling alley. Frank went outside with the infant Joe in his arms and fell down. Neighbors, with that innate, Italianesque love for children, scolded him.

Joe, the infant, was probably thrilled. Every fourth of July was a big event to him. As an adult he bought firecrackers for all of his children as well as children of friends and relatives. In addition, he provided for a big holiday feast catering all kinds of festive food, turkey, chicken, meatballs, ravioli, spaghetti, sausage, etc. One fourth of July to exhibit his explosive spirit he threw a firecracker through the window of the Alhambra Bowling Alley where his friends were playing poker. He was arrested and spent the night in jail, but he and his friends had a good laugh.

When Joe was three years old, my mother took him, Phil, and Tommy to the bus station when Frank was at work. And, just like that, they left him, departing for Reno, Nevada.

She had enough of Frank's drunkenness and abuse; so she decided to go west and obtain a divorce. From Reno she went to Sacramento, California, marrying my father, Nick Tripodi. My father was strict, being unreasonably so to his step-children while doting on me, his only son. I was four years younger than Joe, who like his sister and brother loved me, but felt ambivalent due to the preferential treatment I received from my father. I vividly remember one dinner when we had horse beans as the major vegetable. Joe hated them, but my father insisted that he eat them. Joe, as ever quick witted, pretended that he ate them and put them in his pocket. He discarded them after dinner.

Joe essentially tolerated Nick. He was never afraid of him even though Nick freely gave spankings with his hands or a belt to all of us. At a young age Joe had an extraordinary love for life. He shined shoes when he was six years old, and sold newspapers and magazines for spending money. It wasn't long before he began to lag pennies, and Joe the gambler was born. He was never religious. He didn't talk about God, nor did he go to church. His religion was gambling, and his Bible was soon to be the Racing form where he would discern the odds on the horse races.

My father was very sick with leukemia from 1939 to 1941, when he died. Joe put up with my father until he was twelve years old; then my father was hospitalized in a variety of places from Sacramento to San Francisco, courtesy of the Western Pacific Railroad where he was employed. In 1940 Frank Torchia died, and Joe lost his true father. My mother, Phil, Joe and I traveled by train to Ithaca, New York for the funeral. I was seven and Joe was eleven. Ironically, seven and eleven are winning numbers in craps and what shooters wish for, "7 come 11." It was on the train where it became clear how competitive Joe was. I had a watch, and he taught me how to tell time. My mother packed food for our three-day trip, and the food had to be rationed. Joe and I would have contests to determine who could go the longest, holding on to his sandwich, without eating. The victor would gloat about how good the sandwich was, while the loser would frown and say something like "no fair." The other game was that of rapidly calling out the sum of extended fingers, e.g., two fingers for Joe and one for me would be three. The victor got to punch the other, a boy's game of controlled violence.

In Ithaca, New York I didn't attend the funeral, but my mother, sister and brother did. There was no talk of the funeral. Joe never discussed his father with me. I was his little brother who could only compete in boys' games. He was stubborn and patient, but so was I. In a contest or a game, he'd never discuss his strategy. Little did I know that he was preparing for a life of gambling where bluffing was as much a strategy as a skill. In Ithaca the game was to see how many glasses of water doused with salt and pepper one could drink. I usually won that game, but I think he tricked me into believing it was a good thing to drink a lot of water sprinkled with salt and pepper. The winner, obviously, had to go to the bathroom much more than the loser. Girl relatives fawned over Joe, who was very good looking, with black wavy hair, hazel-green eyes, a lean body and freckles. As a young boy, he was very clever and able to conceal his true feelings. These were traits he kept throughout his life. He was able to keep secrets. Joe also had a temper and a mean streak, but I didn't learn about them until my father died. Not once did he discuss his feelings with me, but that was understandable since I was his *little brother*. It's the *Big Brother* who is imbued with wisdom and the ways of the world.

# THE SAILBOAT

Christmas is a special time for families and their children and is celebrated in many ways. The centerpiece of Italian-American celebration
is food and drink, interspersed with church attendance and loud conversation. Overtly religious or not, family members go to church at
least twice a year—on Easter and at Christmas. Perhaps, it's due to the
fact that big banquets are held on those days which are devoted to the
spring hunt for Easter eggs and the opening of presents for children at
Christmas.

Prior to my father's death in the late 1930's, Christmas was a joyous
occasion. My mother cooked most of the day and night before Christmas. We would have huge amounts of food on Christmas Eve as well
as on Christmas day. She would buy a pig, and make sausages, pickled
pig's feet, roast pork, and other delicacies. In addition, she would make
chicken soup, roast turkey, chicken cooked in wine, roast potatoes,
eggplant, zucchini fried with eggs, fishes, sardines, cod fish (the famous
baccala of Italian song), and a variety of deserts, biscuits, cookies, etc.
There was too much food, and it was impossible to eat everything,
even with the commanding chant of my mother and father, "Mangia!
Mangia!" ("Eat! Eat!").

The Christmas after my father died in 1941 was not the same.
World War II was declared after the Japanese bombed Pearl Harbor. I
was nine years old. Listening to the radio with my sister, I heard that
many people were worried that the West coast of the United States
might be attacked by the Japanese. I was afraid and told my sister, "It's
a good thing my father died; for he's safe in heaven." The statement
made no sense other than that I thought we might be killed and that I
loved my father. It was a time of anxiety and tenseness. Soon my
brother Tommy would enter the U.S. Navy, and my sister would
marry. My mother, an Italian alien, began to worry that she might have
to be detained in a camp like many Japanese living in California. The
unholy alliance of Germany, Japan, and Italy as the Axis, the foe, in

World War II, sparked the urge in my mother to quickly seek to become a naturalized U.S. citizen. Not only were there fears of war, but also we were poor. My father's long hospitalization depleted any financial resources my mother had. She did not hold a job, but in 1942 she would obtain two jobs so she could feed and clothe us, to rise out of poverty. There was no joyous Christmas in 1941. My mother was still grieving over my father's death, and she was destitute, receiving relief in kind from the welfare office. Christmas presents were clothes that we needed, high-top shoes and socks for me.

There was much sadness in our household that Christmas, but there was one ray of glimmering happiness. This was sparked by my brother Joe. Newspapers in many cities across the United States developed schemes such as letters to Santa Claus to provide a way of giving toys to needy children. The *Sacramento Bee* had a letters-to-Santa-Claus campaign, which began near Thanksgiving and ended just before Christmas. My brother Joe took it upon himself to write a letter to Santa Claus, describing our situation—poverty, the death of my father, and the fact that my mother was raising four children, aged 9, 13, 18, and 19.

Presents were delivered to our house by the *Sacramento Bee*, the evening newspaper. Somehow, I thought my brother Joe got Santa Claus to deliver the presents to the offices of the *Sacramento Bee*, which in turn delivered them to us. I was really amazed to see the letter to Santa Claus in the newspaper. I was happy because I received a toy sailboat.

The sailboat was the biggest toy I ever had. It had to be sailed in a big body of water, so I took it to McKinley Park, about one-and-a-half miles from our house. It was an adventure. I finally put it in the pond at McKinley Park and moved it around with a string. The sailboat introduced me to McKinley Park. There was the Clunie Swimming Pool, baseball diamonds, fields for playing football, basketball courts, and the library. The sailboat led to fantasy. I imagined I was on the boat going to many ports of the world. I couldn't quite reconcile

World War II in my fantasies. I didn't think about the danger of torpedoes and attacks by the Axis. I imagined that I was sailing in tranquil waters in sunny, serene places. My brother Joe thought I should do more than fantasize. He thought I should learn how to fish. I didn't like to eat fish and saw no purpose in trying to catch fish. Joe told me about the basics. Get a long branch from a tree as a pole, some string, a hook, and worms. He didn't stay with me to show me how to do it. In respect to Joe, I tried. I had a makeshift pole, one fishhook that Joe gave me and some string. I dug a hole and found some worms. Disgusting as it was, I put a worm on the hook. I cast the line into the pond and waited. After an hour or so, I thought I should give up the sport of fishing. But, to my surprise, I caught a fish. It was rainbow colored. In no way could I eat that fish. I took the fish off the hook, threw it back in the pond, and ended my very brief career as a fisherman. For serenity and feelings of quiet contentment, my fantasies about sailing on the sailboat were sufficient, with its blue bottom and white sails. It was the fact that Joe was responsible for getting the toys from the *Sacramento Bee* that made me feel he was invincible and could obtain whatever he wanted, even if he had to write a letter to get his way. I'll always remember that sailboat as a simple but loving act of kindness from my brother Joe.

# THE MERCHANT MARINE

World War II intensified from 1942 through 1945. Those were the years in which our family became disrupted. Tommy didn't want to go in the army, particularly the infantry on the front lines; for the risk of death appeared to be higher than in the Navy and Air Force. He actually wanted to be in the U.S. Coast Guard, patrolling waters off the United States of America. However, he did not meet one of the requirements. Disappointed, he enlisted in the U.S. Navy. My brother Tommy was sent to the South Pacific and drove small boats in waters near Australia and New Guinea. There were many tense situations in that area of the world. But what I remember when Tommy returned to America after the war were his pictures of night life, which he seemed to enjoy, in Sydney, Australia. Since Tommy was away during those years, he had little influence on my brother Joe and me. My sister worked as a secretary and was an outstanding worker, well-organized, fast and efficient in typing and other clerical tasks. Joe was usually out, trying to make money and spending what he had on young women and his car. My mother tried to get him to do work around the house, yard work or painting. Her efforts failed because Joe always found the right time to slip away. He probably had more contact with our sister than anyone else. Phil was the oldest sibling, and she was the focal point of responsibility and stability in the family. Everyone would turn to her if there were problems, hurts, or sensitivities aroused by the conditions in which we were living. She was married and lived away from the house on 24th and C Streets. Consequently, she wasn't available much of the time.

My mother was struggling to make money. She had the idea to buy houses and rent them. She worked toward this goal and achieved it in the post-war years. During the war she worked for the Southern Pacific railroad and at the cannery. On weekends, during the spring and summer, she'd take me with her as she went on jobs to pick peaches or strawberries. People were paid by the number of crates they filled. My mother was the second fastest picker, not being able to surpass Rosa, the champion.

Since my mother was worried about citizenship, she enrolled in an evening adult education class at Sutter Junior High School, the infamous "crime school" that I attended in the middle of the World War II years. She took me as a companion to the class, which was filled with foreigners from many different countries. Most of them were middle-aged and older, and no one seemed to be able to speak English very well. They were to learn about the constitution, the number of senators and representatives, ages to be eligible to run for president, and so forth. In addition to class discussion, the students were given homework. Essentially they were being coached so they could pass the citizenship test. Our mother had an excellent memory and memorized the answers to a variety of questions. My mother eventually passed her citizenship examination and was sworn in as an American citizen. She then concentrated on working as much as possible. This meant that both Joe and I were unsupervised during the war.

While World War II inspired Joe to think of ways he could make money through gambling and selling items that were hard to get at inflated prices, it led my friends and me to play war games. There was a dirt hill and a deep hole in a vacant area about three blocks away from my house. First we would choose sides and play war, throwing dirt clouds at each other. This was soon changed to rubber gun wars. The guns were made out of wood which had notches on them. Rubber bands were stretched to desirable notches and fired. Again, the weapons were elevated to bee bee guns, and we shot bee bees at each other. Many of our scenes were re-creations of World War II battles. Fortunately, no one was injured seriously. In the summers a group of us would go to the American River and swing out on a rope tied to a tree over the river and jump. There were many agricultural fields that we traversed to get to the river. We picked tomatoes and peaches, which served as lunch as we explored the river, swimming in whirl pools, and jumping off of bridges. One part that wasn't so relaxing was the day when a farmer shot at us for picking tomatoes.

Once in a while Joe would give me money to go to the movies. I received no allowance, so I got a paper route for the *Sacramento Bee*. I looked older than I was; hence, I passed for 12 years old, the required age, when I was 11. My newspaper route was in the worst part of Sacramento, filled with prostitutes, pimps, and alcoholics. Collecting was a little scary, for I saw people in various states of dress and sobriety. Many of them were slow in paying. Some were threatening, ready to be physical.

It was in these conditions of carefree, unsupervised adolescence during a war which captured the enthusiasm of young and old that Joe at 15 years of age decided to join the Merchant Marine. It wasn't the desire to sail the seas and visit strange sounding places that inspired him. It was the chance to make money. He lagged pennies at high school and was involved in crap games. It wasn't enough for him. School was a bore, so he dropped out. Joe heard that the seamen got extra pay if they sailed in dangerous war zones. The Merchant Marine seemed to him like an opportunity waiting to be realized. The problem was that he wasn't old enough.

Joe reasoned that he could never get our mother to lie for him, nor would she want him to endanger his life. He could get in, however, by a good line of gab, a changed birth certificate, and a forged signature of my mother's. He bought ink eradicator, pens, and a lot of paper. I served as observer for him as to whether or not his forgery looked like my mother's signature. He practiced for hours and hours. I remember getting tired as he constantly asked, "How does that look now?" Finally he felt like he got it right. He erased the year of his birth and changed it so he'd be the correct age and wrote my mother's signature on a form he had. The miracle man, Joe, succeeded again. He got into the Merchant Marine, and he set out to sea. Joe became a cabin boy and on the ship he had access to all sorts of supplies. He sold cake for $1.00 a slice; he lagged pennies, and he started a crap game, as well as betting anybody about anything. The result was that he'd return from a trip with thousands of dollars. In addition, he had a black market mentality. He would bring home fifty cartons of cigarettes and fifty cartons of gum. He sold most of the gum and cigarettes to people in Sacramento. He saved some for himself and gave me a few packs of gum.

Joe went on several trips, each time bringing home money, cigarettes, and gum. I suppose, but don't really know, that he was beginning to perfect his gambling skills. Among his skills were an ability to understand the psychology of men, what they'd do under pressure, and the self awareness to assess his own ability to keep his emotions in check while conning people into making wagers with him that they couldn't win.

He certainly was a hero to me during those years. Naturally, I started to smoke in emulation of Joe. It was right after the war when Tommy was home, and I was caught smoking at a baseball game that Tommy, Joe, and my mother spanked me for smoking. The net effect of that was that I didn't smoke again 'til college.

Although I received little supervision Joe always seemed to know what I was doing, with whom I was playing, and where I had been. He constantly reminded me to stay out of trouble. I suspect that he told certain people he knew to look out for me. One day at the baseball park at 28th and C Streets, I jumped off the backstop and got my shoe caught in a wire. Instead of landing on my feet, I fell on my arm and broke it. Jack Brady, one of the leaders of the C Street Gang and reputed to be one of the toughest, lived across the street from the park. He got to me right away, telling me he knew Joe and would take care of me. Jack took me to the hospital. My arm was broken and put in a cast. Jack was very kind to me. Like many others in the C Street Gang, he eventually spent time in prison for armed robbery. Many like the Herrera brothers were boxers and also into narcotics, which my brother Joe evidently avoided.

Joe seemed to know everyone. He made friends easily, and he also supplied them with cigarettes and other items like liquor. He learned how to attract large numbers of people to engage in gambling. In essence, he developed skills in the Merchant Marine which would help him in developing a clientele for betting on horses. He was a very tough, worldly kid of fifteen years who seemed to enjoy World War II more than anyone I knew. His expertise at gambling was developing rapidly.

# THE BOWLING ALLEY

In adolescence and young adulthood it is quite common to "hang out" at some focal place, typically for recreational activity. Some prefer a street corner; others, a church, cafe, or bar; and still others, pool halls, community centers, clubs, and so forth. Joe "hung out" at the Alhambra Bowling Alley. Bowling alleys serve many functions and are seen differently depending on one's perspective. The Alahambra Bowl consisted of lockers, a number of bowling lanes, a restaurant-cafe, a bar, a game room for card games, and offices for the management. People came to bowl, to have fun, and to compete in league competition. Singles came to the bar or bowled as a way to meet others, to be "picked up" for sex. There were regulars who went to the bar for their daily nourishment from alcohol. There also were those who gambled at the bar, the pool room, or the card room. Couples went on dates to the bowling alley. Many went to the restaurant to get a bite to eat. Some were carrying on affairs and used the bowling alley as a meeting place. Most of the patrons combined bowling, eating and drinking. Another set of customers, prominent businessmen, doctors, lawyers, etc., were interested in gambling for the high stakes in poker games. And, there were small-time gamblers who rolled dice for drinks or money and placed bets on billiard games.

The Alhambra Bowling Alley was to my sister, a place where she and other women played competitively. Phil was among the top women bowlers in the city of Sacramento. She bowled for Bercut Richards, and their team won city championships and competed state wide and nationally. One year she won the City championship for women. During the competition, my brother Joe watched her like a hawk, cheering for every pin knocked down. Phil thought it strange that Joe should watch her so closely because he hadn't been that surveillant previously. She finally found out why. Joe had bet over $2,000 on her to win. He won several thousand dollars, ordering drinks on the house to celebrate my sister Phil's win. Sometimes Phil took me to the bowling alley to keep her eye on me while she bowled. She ordered grilled cheese sandwiches for us to eat. I can still recall the taste of the melted cheese and the aroma of the toasted bread.

The Alhambra Bowling Alley was Joe's work, school, and home away from home. Joe began work setting pins in the frames so they would be lined up for the bowlers. He did this for approximately two years before he enlisted in the Merchant Marine. I went with him and watched him work. He was fast and efficient, and he enjoyed working for money. In addition, he learned to bowl. His bowling average was over 200 which was exceptional for an adolescent. Although Joe was a natural athlete, he wasn't interested enough in any sport to practice the self discipline that leads to athletic supremacy. I was a spectator, not a player. Everybody at the bowling alley liked Joe. He would buy hamburgers and cokes for me and ask me to watch something of his, like a wallet or a sweater while he bowled, worked, or went to different parts of the bowling alley to talk to people.

Joe disliked high school intensely. He gambled, playing craps for lunches from the frats, the wealthier kids. One day he was so bored at school that he jumped out of the window of a classroom and ran off. He never went back. The bowling alley, both before and after he was in the Merchant Marine, was his school. It's where he learned how to gamble. He played with small time gamblers at the bar, shaking the dice in games of Liar's Dice or Poker Dice. He played for drinks or money, instinctively knowing the odds for obtaining various combinations and patterns of dice. Joe also learned the game of pool. Having perfected his skills in bowling and in pool, Joe would bet on his performance. He might bet one person ten dollars that he could shoot a "3" ball in the pocket of the southwest corner on the one hand and bet one hundred dollars he would bowl a strike on the other hand. His brand of cigarettes, Lucky Strikes, exemplified his bowling; he was usually lucky in bowling strikes.

The more serious lessons he learned were about poker and the daily racing form. He was befriended by Johnny Bascou, the owner of the bowling alley, and Butch Nisetich, Sacramento's biggest gambler. Butch was like a father, and Johnny was like an uncle. He very proudly introduced me to them as if they were his parents who were definitely close to royalty. They included him in their poker and pinochle games, teaching him the rules as well as the odds. When Joe was twenty years old, he had his tonsils removed and went right from the hospital to the bowling alley. Joe had a run of 100 aces in pinochle and was so excited that he broke stitches from his tonsillectomy and began to hemorrhage. He was taken to the hospital and was instructed to "take it easy."

Joe may or may not have learned about horse racing and book making from Butch Nisetich. Rumor has it that he did. Since Butch had no children of his own, he treated Joe like a son. Perhaps, he was grooming Joe to take over some of his book making operations. Whether or not that's true, it was clear that Butch was instructing him in probability, chance, the psychology of gambling, and the pragmatics of horse racing.

Joe was a quick learner. He learned the intricacies of the games rapidly. Blessed with an extraordinary memory and a head for quickly calculating odds, he mastered whatever he was interested in. It was a great deal of perseverance, practice, and patience that helped him to judge people: those who were gullible or "born suckers"; those who would cheat any time; those who were extremely skilled; and those who were straight. It was Butch Nisetich, by treating Joe as a son, who gave him the basic foundation of caring. That enabled Joe to learn something about the psychology of other gamblers. And, it was the bowling alley that served as a haven for him while he was a gambling apprentice.

# THE BAKERY

Joe had another job in addition to gambling at the Alhambra Bowling Alley. He was an apprentice cake decorator at Channel Pie Bakery from the ages of seventeen to twenty one. A cake decorator should be artistic, creative, and dexterous with excellent eye-hand coordination. Joe had all of those attributes as well as speed. He could create a new design and implement it on the cake with icing in various colors and patterns.

When I was fourteen, jobs were not hard to obtain in the summer. Joe said he could get me a job where he worked. On my first day at Channel Pie, I had the task of taking pies off a conveyor belt and loading them into boxes on a cart. The pies would keep coming, so one had to be fast enough to load the pies, turn the cart around to load more pies, take them off the conveyor belt, etc. I was slow! Pies started to fly all over the place, landing on the floor. I was transferred to another job in the bakery, but not before I saw what was done with pies that fell on the floor. They were scooped up, and the ingredients went into other pies. So the pies were filled with dirt and any other objects that happened to be loose. Nevertheless, I ate some of the pies. Joe told me which ones were good. Tarts with lemon or apple were the best. They were delicious. It was obvious that I was better at eating the pies than loading them. The next job at the bakery was one in which I washed pots and cleaned the floors, hosing them down with water. I worked alone at my own speed, and from time to time I'd eat a small pie or some hot bread.

During the Channel Pie years, Joe drove a green Cadillac convertible, which was his signature car for the next decade, i.e. a new Cadillac convertible every year, with the exception of the year in which he drove a lavender 1954 Thunderbird convertible. He and his friends would drive around as if they owned the city, making remarks at other drivers and pedestrians. On one occasion a driver bumped the rear fender of Joe's Cadillac. One of Joe's friends was annoyed. He asked Joe to stop in front of the car. His friend got out and started to argue with the driver. Thereupon a fight started, the cops came, and Joe was arrested for being an accessory to a fight. He and his friends laughed about it. They were tough guys and thought they could do anything. It was one of these tough guys, Babe Bua, that for a time was a suspect in Joe's murder.

While working at Channel Pie, Joe was still enrolled in the school of gambling at the bowling alley. He was learning that cheaters shouldn't be allowed to get away with anything. If they did, the gambler would lose respect. Joe interpreted this to mean, "You beat them up! You use your fists." An incident occurred at a carnival that was a short distance from Channel Pie. A carnival worker managed a game, the object of which was to guess which shell had a pea underneath it. The game went on, and Joe was losing $300. All of a sudden, realizing something wasn't right, Joe stopped the game. He asked to see the pea. The fact of the matter was there was no pea. Joe and his friends virtually started a riot and didn't leave until Joe recovered all of his money. They used their fists and got their way. Perhaps, Butch Nisetich should have explained to Joe that he personally didn't have to use his fists. There were other ways to get the best of a cheater. It was also evident that Joe needed to control his temper to a greater extent if he wished to fill the image of the cool gambler fazed by nothing and focused only on the game at hand. However, Joe was also an adolescent, not quite having achieved the maturity of later years.

Joe lived at our sister Phil's house in the Oak Park area. He was involved in gambling most of each night, and he slept late, often missing work at Channel Pie. One day the owner of the bakery who valued Joe's skills as a cake decorator sent a taxi to pick up Joe. This was right after Joe made up the story that his car wasn't working. From then on my sister took it upon herself to wake up Joe every morning. She would wake him up, and he'd fall back to sleep. She subsequently changed her strategy so that she would see him leave for work each morning. Later she found out that he didn't go to work, he left to develop his gambling skills and to cavort with his girlfriend, Shirley.

Joe really seemed to care for Shirley. She might have been the first real love of his life. He used to brag about how nice she was, how good she looked, and how much class she had. Her father, a golf professional, probably thought that Joe was beneath his daughter's class. Joe and Shirley broke up, but nobody knew why. It was a very low class thing of her father when he told people he didn't want to go to Joe's funeral because he didn't want to be associated with that dago, that guinea, that hood. The shadow of the Mafia and the prejudice towards Italian Americans engulfed that golf pro. Rumor had it that he himself was a cheater.

Phil was hoping that Joe would be a full-fledged cake decorator and make lots of money for overtime work, for which he'd be paid time and a half. Joe had different ideas. As he approached the goal of Cake Decorator, he became less interested in that way of life. Joe liked freedom and the opportunity to keep his own hours, night and day. He didn't want an 8 to 5 job. Joe announced to one and all that he was retiring from cake decorating. He really meant that he was going into business for himself. He would be a full-time gambler.

To celebrate his retirement at the bakery, Joe decorated a cake and shared it with everyone working there. In a sense, he was saying that "The cake's on me." This was similar to his buying drinks for everyone and saying, "The drinks are on me." When Joe felt good he celebrated his momentary happiness by offering food and drink to one and all.

When he retired at twenty one, I was in college. I became more and more distant from Joe as I plunged into my studies. I carried with me many of Joe's teachings that were formed at the bakery. "Go to the dentist often to check your teeth." "Don't gamble." It was as if Joe wanted to be sure I took care of myself and avoided illegal activities. Joe also gave advice that I didn't follow. "Act as if you have money, even if you don't." "Wear good clothes, and drive an expensive car. It makes people think you're wealthy. That way they'll respect you." It was respect that Joe seemed to be looking for, by having more money than others and by being tougher than those around him. Yet, he was aware at a young age that he really had a desire for a simpler life where people would respect him for what he did, who he was, and what he stood for. Gambling was to be for him a compulsion as well as his profession. In the next decade, his 20s and 30s, Joe became a high roller, gambling and losing thousands of dollars at Lake Tahoe, in addition to making thousands of dollars at book making, dice, and poker in Sacramento. His life became rather removed from decorating cakes.

# *Family*

# MOTHER

Our mother immigrated to the United States of America when she was in her early 20's. She only had a third grade education, but she was literate in Italian. She also had all the skills of a peasant woman. She could grow food in gardens, make sausage and various meats from pigs, bake bread, cook huge meals for many people, make wine, embroider, make clothes, sew, etc. The town she lived in is about 2,000 feet in elevation. It is a very small village, San Pietro d'Apostolo, in the province of Calabria. The church in the town was built by her grandfather. Legend has it that he was accused of murder, and he vowed to God he would build a church should he be acquitted. He was freed, and he indeed designed and built the village church. He was a priest, but earthly desires prevailed, with him marrying my great-grandmother who was a nun.

My mother worked hard in America. In Ithaca, she performed her duties as housewife and mother. Life must have been very difficult for her to have tolerated a great deal of abuse from Frank Torchia and to have decided to leave him and go west with Joe, Tommy, and Phil. Perhaps she thought there would be improvement in her situation after she married my father and settled in Sacramento, California. As we grew up in the depression years and the later 1930's, we witnessed her daily struggles. She worked hard managing her family. Often she would take me on walks to the river, sometimes picking mushrooms. She argued frequently and was very unhappy. When friends visited, however, she acted differently, conversing easily and recalling events and conditions in Italy that no one else seemed to remember.

After my father died, our mother exerted a great deal of energy in managing the household, working in two jobs, and saving money to invest in apartment buildings. Phil and Tommy, the older and more responsible ones, helped her a great deal. Joe disappeared to avoid the endless number of projects she devised.

She saw to it that we were clothed and fed. My mother also had her own life. She married again in the middle 40's to a man who appeared to have money. Perhaps, that's why she married him. He had a huge house, and my mother and I moved there. Joe and Tommy were in the war, and Phil lived away with her husband. I liked Mr. Mandella. He seemed nice and had a goat which ate everything in sight but still allowed me to pet him. After one month or less my mother decided to divorce him.

My mother prospered and managed to buy several small apartment houses to rent. She had sugar diabetes for which she had to take insulin shots daily. In spite of her illness, she was a strong-willed, self-determined woman. When the house we lived in needed a new foundation, she would figure out how to do it. She'd have her children do the heavy work. I recall helping her erect steps made out of plaster.

I don't know the real reasons my mother wouldn't let Joe live with us after his stint in the Merchant Marine. I was in junior high school. I suspect that he wasn't giving her enough money. She knew he was making more money than he indicated.

Joe teased her about money because he knew she respected it like he did and that she would take as much as she could get. One day he asked her if she wanted to go to Italy. She said, "Yes." Joe took out a wad of money and burned a bill right in front of her. He laughed. She was extremely angry. Joe displayed his cruel streak, probably a vindication of the possibility she threw him out because he didn't give her enough money. Joe made up for it later, paying for a trip to Italy for her. It was a kindness that she remembered to her dying day.

# SIBLINGS

Joe loved his sister Phil. As in many Italian families she, because she was the oldest female, was responsible for taking care of her brothers. Her responsibilities grew when my father died and when my mother was ill. Phil was Joe's *Big Sister*, and she looked out for him. She loved him.

Both Tommy and Joe worked at odd jobs to make extra money. They were supposed to give what they made to my mother. Tommy, reliable and compliant, did so. Joe, who was eleven years old, gave up one dollar out of every five he made. What he did with the extra four dollars was to spend it on gambling or hide it in the basement. The basement was a wine cellar which contained three barrels of homemade wine each year. After my father was ill and died, my mother still carried on the wine-making tradition. I used to go downstairs to sneak wine out of the barrels. Joe went down to dig a hole in the dirt floor` to hide his money.

Joe started gambling by going to the old public market to lag coins. The object of coin lagging was to see which of the coins tossed was closest to the backstop. The one that had the closest coin won, taking all the other coins that were thrown. Joe developed that skill at a very early age, hardly ever losing. But Joe was afraid his sister would find out. While she was watching to see if he was staying out of trouble, he was eyeing her to determine whether or not she knew about the extra money he was hiding.

When Joe was seventeen years old, my mother kicked him out of her house. They argued a great deal. He did not want to do any chores although he gave her money. Joe moved in with Phil who converted a garage into a room for him. She had married Aubrey Halsted, and both of them completely accepted Joe and his behaviors. Joe was up all hours of the night, drinking, scheming, and gambling.

Joe was forever grateful to his sister Phil for taking him in when he had no place to go. When he was in his 20's he became quite successful in terms of making money. He gave money to my sister so she could purchase a house. Phil had a special room attached to the house, and that room was for Joe. Joe was extremely proud of it. He showed off the house and the room, and he brought friends there to play cards. He also played pinochle with my sister and her husband. He used the room after he bought his own house and was living there with his first wife Mary and her two children. The room served as a sanctuary and a reminder that his sister Phil would always have a place for him.

In my sister's eyes Joe was a retired cake decorator at 21, reputed to have been very artistic and well respected, and a confirmed gambler who was generous to his family. Yet she would worry about him, whether he'd get in trouble or get hurt by some of the characters with whom he gambled. She knew he was anxious about some of the losses he incurred, but he always seemed to recover. He also had a temper, for he simply didn't like to lose money. One time he went to play craps and blackjack at Lake Tahoe on the Nevada side where gambling was legal. He was so angry when he was losing that he tipped a card table over, rushed out of the casino, and took a taxi from Lake Tahoe to Sacramento. Phil knew that Joe wasn't always patient, and that losing frustrated him.

As a kind of diversion my sister was involved with Joe in a football pool, collecting predicted scores from a number of people throughout the city. It was a time when things were good. The money was flowing, and the living was easy. However, there were rough times ahead.

My sister, Aubrey, and their family, two girls and a boy, spent a period of time living in fear. There were always people attempting to rob Joe. He carried large sums of money on him, and he often hid money in his house or my sister's house. Two years before his death, Joe received a tip from a friend of his on the police force that a group led by an ex-con was going to try to kidnap my sister and possibly her youngest daughter, Toni Ann. Joe told my sister about it, telling her to "shut up" and be calm (as if that could be possible) when detectives would be with them. For two weeks my sister and her family were escorted or followed by detectives wherever they went. Detectives lived at her house in eight-hour shifts. Anxiety and fear were the prevailing moods, and Toni Ann was to relive those fears for many years later. The group of people were caught and convicted, and the kidnap threat was over. But the fear and anxiety persisted. Joe was robbed several times after that episode. The last robbery culminated in his death. There were also good times in the two years preceding his death. He had a son Joey from his second wife Janice, and a daughter Maria from his third wife Jeanne with whom he was living in a large ranch house with huge acreage and horses to ride. My sister and Aubrey recounted how generous he was to them. Joe owned part of a restaurant, The Buggy Whip, and he employed relatives, children and adults, to do various chores. He saw to it that Phil and Aubrey were constantly supplied with food for their family. They had choice meats, hamburger, vegetables, fruits, desserts, and breads. On the Halloween before his death Joe surprised Phil and her family. He set up a big buffet with pumpkins, seafood, crab, lobster, and varieties of meats. After they ate, Joe, as if he were the Pied Piper, led all the children on a trick or treat excursion. It would be hard to imagine that anyone would refuse to buy treats for those kids, who were led by a person regarded as "bigger than life" by both children and adults.

Aubrey and Phil were animated as they recently recalled their life with Joe. Aubrey said it was difficult for them to adjust after Joe's death. Not only did they lose Joe's love and friendship, they also lost the weekly supply of food and wine. They had to change their lifestyle. They were also angry. They felt the investigation of his murder was incomplete. Aubrey said that two girls who lived with Garcia, the accused killer, were going to testify at his trial. They left town, however, when they received a call that they would be killed if they testified. Aubrey said he could talk about Joe for hours and hours, thus verifying the Sacramento newspaper columnists' assertions about people playing parlor games attempting to discover the killer.

Phil, loyal to the end, still brings flowers to the vault in which Joe is entombed. She prays for him and for our mother who is entombed next to Joe. Phil never did speak to Babe Bua after he was jailed and released. Although he was supposed to be Joe's friend, he stole money from The Buggy Whip where he was maitre d'. She still believes he was involved in setting up robberies of Joe's money. He died a decade ago, certainly not missed by my sister. Phil was a dutiful, loving and loyal sister. She still makes room for Joe in her heart and in her mind.

Tommy was not as close to Joe as his sister Phil, but he regarded Joe as close family, loving him like an Italian brother should. Whereas Joe was steeped in the world of gambling, Tommy was immersed in baseball, another way for second-generation Italian-Americans to try to strike it rich in America, the so-called land of opportunity. Tommy began his career playing for an American Legion team while he was of high school age. He was relatively short for a ball player, five feet, eight inches tall, but he was powerful, able to hit the home run ball. Joe would stop by to watch Tommy play for an American Legion team in various ball parks in Sacramento, 21st and C Street, McKinley Park, 28th and C Street, Land Park and so forth. Like many other athletes, Tommy's career was interrupted during World War II. He enlisted in the Navy and spent most of his time in Australia and New Guinea, driving P.T. boats and serving as a Navy Commando. Hence, Tommy was away during Joe's formative teen years when Joe learned more about gambling and life in the fast lanes, bowling and otherwise.

Joe tried to get Tommy to invest in a small business, offering to get him started. However, while Joe was a risk taker and an entrepreneur, Tommy was not. I remember Joe talking to Tommy about setting up a small railroad for tourists at the local zoo in Land Park. The idea was offered before such train rides became popular fixtures across the country. Tommy didn't want to take the risk.

As Joe prospered in the restaurant business, he hired Tommy to do odd jobs. For a period of time it was Tommy who took the restaurant receipts to his house. Ironically, Joe changed the procedure several months before his death, and he himself took the receipts home.

Tommy is a good person. He was loyal to Joe, and he tried from time to time to offer him advice for staying out of trouble. He too loved Joe and was grateful for the banquets and food delicacies that Joe shared with Tommy's and Phil's families. Tommy lives in the house my mother and I lived in before she died, one block away from Phil's house. It's fitting that Tommy lives in his mother's house, which is now his. Legend has it that Tommy was the most Italian of Christina's sons, not being weaned until he was five years old. In later life he always doted on her and expected everyone else to do the same.

Joe's relationship with me, his little brother, developed after my father died. It was the beginning of World War II, and my brother Tommy had enlisted in the Navy. Joe was beginning to work at making money through odd jobs and gambling. I was very quiet, rarely talking at family gatherings. We were poor. My mother would take me to the welfare office to prove I existed and to carry the box of groceries we received from Mary Judge (she indeed judged us!), the social investigator. We received what was then called "relief in kind" rather than cash benefits. My mother didn't stay on welfare long. Since there was a war, many jobs were available for women. She obtained two jobs, a daytime job at the Southern Pacific Railroad as a custodian, and a nighttime job at the Cannery, canning peaches and other fruits for Del Monte. This meant that I hardly saw her. Since I was alone frequently, I relished any contact with my brother Joe. I worshiped him, but I knew I was regarded as different. Joe, Tommy, and Phil had a different father. I was much darker in complexion than they were. Also, my father was mean to them. Joe exhibited a cruel streak in his relationship with me. He ordered me to do various things for him; and if I didn't do them, he would hit me. Saying, "I'll tell Ma," was of no use since she wasn't available. He completed his domination over me by tying me up and leaving me tied up for hours. The more I cried, the more pleasure he took in laughing. I quickly learned not to cry, to be patient, and to say nothing. These behaviors weren't much fun for Joe, so he untied me. But I was quick to do things for him, shining his shoes, for example. Perhaps, Joe was just vindictive, getting even with my dead father through me. Or, perhaps, euphemistically of course, he was giving me an object lesson in patience. Joe also controlled people by the way he used money. He began to pay me for the chores he asked me to do, thus reinforcing the likelihood that I would continue to do them. This dominant-submissive relationship lasted for several years and diminished rapidly as I entered high school.

I thought of Joe as my protector. I knew if I got into any trouble, he would help me. There was a streetcar that went from 24th and C Street, a block from our house to the downtown area near the Capitol and the park surrounding it about three miles away. For my strange recreation, I used to race the street car to see if I could beat it downtown. Most of the time I lost. The only way I could win was to take short cuts and not exactly follow the street car route. One day I roamed around Capitol Park, and a man gave me a slip of paper which said, "Meet me here at 8:00 p.m." I was so scared that I ran all the way home, beating any street car that dared to overtake me. I showed the note to my brother. He arranged a plan where I would go to meet the man, and if he appeared, Joe would then beat him up. We followed the plan, but the man didn't cooperate. He wasn't there. Nevertheless, Joe's action made me feel protected.

Joe was involved in many schemes to make money. He would take me with him to midget auto races where he had a concession stand for selling cushions. I didn't like shouting, "Pillows here. Pillows here." However, I did, and Joe made money, sharing a small amount with me. Perhaps, he taught me a little bit about salesmanship.

In later years Joe bragged to his friends about my academic achievements. He respected education, and he knew that it was another way to climb up the ladder of social integration in American society. On the other hand, he also was aware that much academic learning is insufficient for preparing one to deal with the problems of life involved with work, family, marriage, sex, money, and so forth.

Joe was concerned about me. He didn't want me to follow in his footsteps. He thought that I shouldn't gamble and be subject to the stresses and strains in that world. I don't like to play cards, and that is due to his teachings. Gambling is a curious phenomenon. It attracts, sucks in, and captures many of us. It is indifferent to social class, ethnicity, and upbringing.

Another lesson that Joe taught me was to go to the dentist regularly. This I have done. When I was a teenager, Joe would give me money to have my teeth examined. I thought it was because of his interest in personal hygiene and the prevention of cavities. However, the dentist, Dr. Wroten, was a friend of his. It was also probable that the dentist owed him money and was paying "in kind," no doubt, as a "professional" courtesy.

Joe knew doctors, lawyers, and other professionals. They often came to his assistance. I never knew for sure, but I had the feeling that Joe was involved in many illegal activities besides gambling. And, I believed that he might possibly have enlisted professional men in those activities. In those days almost all professionals were men. Joe excelled in omertà, the code of silence. It was strange, but I had the feeling, not the knowledge, that my brother was capable of doing anything, illegal or otherwise, to protect members of his family. Even as I myself became a professional, I continued to look up to Joe. I respected him as a human being and as my brother whom I loved.

# WIVES

Joe had a way with women. He was handsome, attentive, direct, and charming. With a huge wad of bills in his pocket and wearing expensive slacks, polo shirts, cardigan sweaters and loafers, Joe had a carefree, romantic quality about him. When he entered a room, he was quickly noticed; he was in charge. Charismatic to the core, both men and women wanted to talk with him, to be seen with him. He spent his money freely, often inviting strangers at a bar to share in his, "The drinks are on me." Women loved to go out with him because he made them feel important. He drove Cadillac convertibles at high speeds, cutting through corner gas stations so he wouldn't have to stop for stop signs or traffic lights.

Joe was a skilled driver, and he would put on driving exhibitions for the women he escorted. At 13 years of age he had his first car, a V-8 black, open-aired, jalopy. The first time he gave me a ride in it, I had my hands on the door as he sped away. The door opened, and I held on to it as I was dragged along the street. He finally stopped, and said, laughing, "You should have shut the door." I learned quickly that he was never at fault; it was always someone or something else.

As a young man he and his friend, Jimmy Wheeler, drove his green Cadillac convertible from California to New York. Wearing dirty Levis, they drove to the Waldorf Astoria in New York City hoping to be treated like royalty since they had money. They were kicked out before they could get in.

My brother Joe would give me money to go to the movies in exchange for washing and waxing his car. He would want it to look nice for his girlfriend, Shirley, the first woman he was serious about. He said, "She had class. She wasn't trash like most of the girls I know." Shirley was the daughter of a professional golfer at William Land Park. I never saw her, but in a picture Joe showed me she appeared to be attractive, a pretty blonde with a good figure. Joe went out with her quite a bit, and he presumably had considered marrying her. It never happened. Perhaps, her father had intervened, seeing Joe as a twenty-year-old punk kid who was too much into gambling. Or, maybe she thought he was too adventurous. Joe never talked about it. All I knew was that was the first time he had mentioned a woman he liked.

Joe kept late hours, gambling, going to bars, booking horses, driving to Lake Tahoe for more gambling, shows, night clubs, and, of course, women. He went out every night, most often ending up with a woman. He knew prostitutes, dancers, show girls, bar maids, ordinary women. Most often he would meet women in restaurants and bars. That's how he met his first wife Mary. She, as were all of his wives, was attractive and caught up in his charisma and carefree attitude. Mary was thin, hazel eyed and red headed. She had two children from a previous marriage, Louie and Sissy. Joe and Mary married and eventually bought a house in the same neighborhood in which Joe's sister and her husband, Aubrey, lived. Mary was very quiet, and she loved Joe a great deal. As they got to know each other, Mary learned about Joe's fears and anxieties. She was afraid that Joe would get hurt someday because of the underworld characteristics of many associated with illegal gambling. Joe kept up his nightly gambling habits. He played in a floating crap game, he took bets at bars; and he played poker. At first Mary was involved in some of his activities, but her involvement diminished considerably. She saw less and less of him. She was lonely and fearful. When he had bad gambling nights, he would go home saturated with heavy doses of beer and Vodka Collins. Joe would check on her activities during the day. Even though he was away, he'd remember what she was supposed to be doing. As he drank more, in his own house where only he and Mary were present, he became abusive. According to Mary, he used to beat her up. Out of frustration, gambling fears, and anxieties, charming, happy-go-lucky Joe took on the behavior of his father who was also abusive to our mother. There are two different, simple versions of how the marriage ended. Mary ostensibly left due to Joe's abusiveness. On the other hand, it was rumored that she had an affair with a gardener; Joe found out, and in true Macho fashion of the

Italian male, he "kicked her out." I felt that Joe loved her and that he was especially fond of her children.

After his divorce from Mary, Joe was introduced to Janice by a friend of his. Janice was bubbly, very intelligent, a vivacious blonde. Joe and Janice were soon married. They lived in the same house that Joe and Mary lived in. Janice quickly learned about his gambling and was involved in calculating odds and taking bets.

Janice had two boxer dogs. On one Memorial Day, the dogs chewed up most of their living room furniture. It was too much for Joe to take, and he didn't relish having the dogs. Nevertheless, he didn't seem overly angry about it. They went to Lake Tahoe often, and they seemed to complement each other. As with Mary, Joe began to spend more and more time away from Janice. He spent more time at home when Louie and Sissy were visiting. Janice was very understanding of Joe's liking of Mary's children, and she helped take care of them. My sister and brother Tommy's wife did not appear to like Janice. They thought she was flaky, a "kook."

In 1961 Janice became pregnant with Joe's son, Joey. Soon after, Joe had an affair with a woman, Jeanne, who eventually became his third wife. According to my sister, Janice left the marriage after she found out about Joe's involvement with Jeanne. Evidently Joe had gone out with other women while Janice was pregnant.

I contacted Janice 25 years after Joe's death, asking for information about her relationship with Joe. Janice was angry and felt that she didn't get a fair divorce settlement. Whereas at the same point in time, Mary indicated he was abusive but she still loved him. In a personal communication Janice wrote (July 9, 1996), "Joe was magnificently boring in that he was predictable. An unloved child grew to become an incredibly self-centered boy/man who left a wake of ruin and pain that never seemed to blot out his own pain/torture."

Joe moved into an apartment with Jeanne. He met her in a bar, and they evidently hit it off quite well. Jeanne was an attractive brunette, with a keen sense of business. They prospered, both in terms of real estate and the restaurant. Jeanne was interested in real estate, and she obtained a real estate license. She had two children, Michael and Susan, from a previous marriage, whom Joe accepted as his own. According to Joe, when he acted as if he were asleep, Jeanne would take money out of his pants pocket. Evidently, if this is true, Joe didn't confront her about this. Jeanne was not cordial toward Joe's son. When she was pregnant with Maria, Joe's daughter, at a Christmas dinner, she yelled out to "stop that kid from crying," according to my sister Phil. Whereas there was enmity between Phil and Jeanne, Jeanne reputedly had a closer relationship with Vera, Tommy's wife, who may have reported Joe's activities to Jeanne.

Joe started going out with women while Jeanne was pregnant. In fact, he moved out for a time, returning to live in the extra room my sister had built for him. Reportedly he was involved with one or two women at the time of his death, and it appeared to be common knowledge among his family.

Joe was engaging with women, and he received their pleasures when he was attentive to them. He never seemed to be happy. Perhaps, he never forgave his mother for leaving his father. And, in turn, when she looked into Joe's taunting eyes, our mother may have been reminded of her guilt at leaving his father.

# CHILDREN

Joe had the Italian love of children. He was kind to all children, giving them food, candy, and money. I believe he was happiest when he saw children smile, easily accepting the love in kind that he offered. Perhaps, he felt unloved as a child, and his gestures were intended to provide a more comforting world of love for children.

Joe loved Louie and Sissy, children of his first wife Mary. He treated them as his own. He exuded kindness and gentleness in their presence. He adored Louie, the red-headed, freckled boy who looked like his mother Mary. He took Louie with him to different places, granting, some would say spoiling him, his every wish. Louie also adored Joe, and he would always comply with his requests. Joe continued to see both children after he and Mary divorced. In Joe's eyes they were his children. Joe took them on expeditions to the American River, showing them how to swim and shoot bee bee guns. At the same time, Joe was a doting uncle to my sister's children, as well as my brother Tommy's. He'd always provided big treats for the kids (that's what he called them) on holidays—firecrackers on the 4th of July, candy and money on Halloween and Thanksgiving, and lavish presents on Christmas.

Joey was, according to my sister, a cute blonde boy who was "full of hell." He was very smart, and was driving, so the story goes, a motorized car at the age of ten. He was over indulged by Joe. Little Joey was the crown prince and could have whatever he wanted.

Joe was tender to his daughter Maria, a black-haired, fragile looking person who had Joe's facial features. She, along with her siblings, were given whatever they wanted. They lived on a ranch, and could go horseback riding on their property which extended for many acres to the American River.

After Joe died there were court proceedings between his wife Jeanne, his ex-wife Janice, and my sister. The deliberations involved the control and use of insurance money for Joey. The money went to Joey, and he, of course, spent it. Joey had problems of substance abuse in the years after Joe's death, and he was sent to prison for selling drugs. The bitterness of Joey's mother about his prison status was expressed to me in a personal communication (July 7, 1996):

> "Do I sound angry? No more than would be expected of any mother whose only son is rotting away in a stinking prison due to the lack of interest by his father's family. Lack of interest is a very polite way of describing the undermining they dished out by reinforcing my non-human status—the constant references to his mother, the 'kook' (relieving his father's responsibility and placing the blame on me, some kind of idiot who was responsible for a fatherless home). The really destructive issue was that this left me with little authority in my son's life. He didn't pay much attention to me when I tried to warn him of the certainty of arrests, etc."

Mary's reaction was different. Her son Louie also was a substance abuser. He currently lives with her, and she mentions little of his substance abuse problems. She is supportive of him and does not blame anyone but Louie for the trouble he has borne.

Maria grew up with her siblings and her cousins, and she seemed to have a relatively normal life. I have no knowledge that she was involved in delinquent activities. She worked, and she married, moving from Sacramento to Los Angeles. Her mother Jeanne also moved to the Los Angeles area. There is no communication between Jeanne and my brother Tommy and sister Phil. Joe, of course, was the focal point of all of these relationships. One could only speculate what might have transpired had Joe still been alive. I suspect he would have continued to dote on his children, hoping that they would have grandchildren whom he could love in his way, giving material objects, money, and indulging smiles. Joe cared for the helpless, and young children are helpless, needing material comforts, nurturing and love. Children, in Joe's eyes, weren't like adults. Children depend on adults, and they need them. Children are appreciative of indulgences on their behalf, and they do respond to kindness and genuine interest in their development. Special relationships, in contrast, as in Joe's situations, can be transitory. They demand mutual respect, love, and hard work for their continuance. Adults in spousal relationships have to give and take to maintain relationships. Joe preferred the one-way dominant relationship of a benevolent parent.

# Gambling

# CRAP GAMES

Most of us have recreational habits. We watch football games on TV while drinking beer, wine, and other liquids to wash down enormous helpings of chips, Nachos, and other kinds of junk food. We read the daily horoscope before breakfast. We jog at a certain time every day. We make small wagers on the outcomes of baseball games. Habits, such as these can become compulsions. A compulsion, according to Webster (Webster's Ninth New Collegiate Dictionary, Merriam Webster Inc. Publishers, Springfield, Massachusetts, 1990, p. 271) is an "irresistible impulse to form an irrational act."

My brother Joe's compulsion was the playing of crap games, wagers, and dice. Even after he made enough money from booking horses, he had to play other games. It was the urge to throw the dice that devoured him. He rolled them in bars and a certain section of old Sacramento. His floating crap games took place in the alleys of the worse parts of town. In the barrios, bars, back rooms, alleys and wherever, Joe had a compulsion to play. Joe liked it most when he was shooting dice with a group of men. They had to keep one eye on the dice, and the other on the police who would arrest them if they could. These floating crap games occurred primarily in the Mexican area. Players would contribute to the pot; and they took turns rolling the dice. Excitement raged. Each player was part chicken, dancing at each throw, cackling his desires, and part hawk, hovering (over the dice) and looking to see that no one was cheating. When Joe won, his eyes bulged, a big grin lit up his face, and his body straightened up. He was on top of the world. When Joe lost, he perspired profusely and became extremely agitated and short-tempered. Then he'd bet double-or-nothing in hopes of recuperating his losses. He'd keep it up until he won or lost so much money that he'd have to stop. Those games were played in the brightness of day as well as in the late hours of the night. After losing, Joe became depressed, but only for a very short period of time. With heavy losses, he'd be momentarily let down, but then he'd seek other ways to make money. He was a man of action, not one to dwell on immediate adversity.

Joe taught me the basics of dice games, informing me that players can cheat in at least three ways. First, the gambler capitalizes on chance. He makes bets where he has a better chance of winning, particularly against one who doesn't know the odds. Second, the odds can be altered by manipulating the dice in the way that they're thrown. Joe had a pair of loaded dice. They always produced a seven. The gambler switches the loaded dice for the dice that are being rolled. Of course, the dice have the same color, e.g. red faces and white dots. The skilled cheater is adept at sleight of hand, being able to change one pair of dice for another without the other player observing the change. Or, the gambler can throw the dice so they aren't spinning, and the same numbers are reproduced; i.e., he makes his point by throwing the dice in such a way that, e.g. by sliding them, the same numbers appear. The wary player, however, insists that the dice be shaken and then rolled. A third way is not a popular way. It was brought to my attention when I read the book, *Six Roads from Newton: Great Discoveries in Physics*, by Edward Speyer (John Wiley & Sons, Inc., New York, 1994). In discussing probability, Speyer used the example of dice, and he recalled for the reader an episode from the Broadway musical, *Guys and Dolls*. Big Jule insisted that Nathan Detroit should use his dice. Nathan pointed out to him that the dice had no spots, but Big Jule said it didn't matter because he remembered them. With a gun held to Nathan's head, he forced Nathan to roll the dice. Big Jule could call out whatever number he wanted. Perhaps, this method was used on my brother Joe when his assailants held a gun to his head while asking him to roll for his life. Joe didn't play. He didn't show them where he hid his money. Joe gambled and lost, shot in the head as he fought for his life. When Joe played dice with me, I was eleven years old. He always won because he knew the odds, and he was able to make me think that there was an even chance for me to win. I thought the dice were like magic, having a power that could lull people into betting and losing. I had no idea about the odds and probability. Joe took advantage of me, capitalizing on chance phenomena. Later, he explained the odds to me as well as he could; but, putting me down at the same time by showing me that I was a sucker, one who could easily be beaten. It was paradoxical. He showed me that I was stupid and incompetent, thus making himself appear superior. In contrast, he was indicating to me that it was stupid to gamble when there were people like him that could make me look like a nitwit.

Joe was once in a crap game where one of the players used a pair of loaded dice. The player was on a run, i.e., consecutive winning throws. At first, Joe didn't think much about it. However, he soon noticed the same combination of three and four occurring. This was a little fishy. Tired of losing, Joe seized the dice the next time a three and a four appeared. Joe threw them down once, rolling three and four. He threw them down again, and three and four came up. The roller was starting to run off. Joe grabbed him, beating him with his fists. Joe took his money back and went off.

Joe was most excited when he was on a run, making his points. At a crap game with seven others in an alley late at night, played under a street lamp, Joe hit eleven straight winners. He was making lots of money, feeling good, shouting louder and louder as he made point after point. So much noise was made that the police in a patrol car heard it, and they zoomed in search of the crap game. The players quickly picked up their money and ran every which way. They eluded the police, but Joe lost some of the money he made in his magnificent run. Joe was more upset about not being able to continue his winning streak than he was about the cops breaking up the crap game.

Games at the produce market were more controlled. The games were tolerated and not broken up very often. Joe always carried red dice with him, being ever ready to "shake 'em and roll 'em." He worked on his skills at Sacramento High School, beating other students in crap games, and in the Merchant Marine where mariners in the war zones were eager to take gambling risks. When Joe played, he energized all the players and bystanders. This was his compulsion, and he was sucking all of those around him into his game so they too would be compelled to play until they couldn't keep their eyes open any longer for lack of sleep. Joe thought he controlled the dice, but in truth they controlled him. He couldn't leave his dice in the same way that he couldn't leave a new love. His lovers were transitory, but his love of dice and gambling was ever-constant, consuming his thoughts night and day.

# POKER

Joe's mentors in poker were Butch Nisetich, Sacramento's illustrious big-time gambler, and Johnny Bascou, owner of the Alhambra Bowling Alley. They took him under their wings and trained him when he was a young teenager setting pins in the bowling alley. Joe learned the rules of the game and a variety of ways to play draw poker. Butch and Johnny also taught Joe the art of bluffing, and they schooled him in the odds of obtaining various hands. Like so many things, it's best to learn by doing. Joe at 17 years of age, was allowed to sit in with the businessmen and professional gamblers, playing poker with Johnny and Butch in the card room of the Alhambra Bowling Alley. Joe brought me to several of those games. I sat next to him and watched. I had never in my short life seen so much money. The room was dimly lit, and the blue haze of cigarette and cigar smoke enshrouded the players. A rancid odor of stale tobacco suffused the room. The players were relatively quiet and very professional, calmly indicating whether they would raise the ante or pass. The pot contained thousands of dollars, a stake that would go to the winner. I didn't understand the game, but I knew the players were intently interested and were risking a great deal of money. Joe probably risked the most since he had no strong base of money for gambling at the time. Joe was tense. Learning how to remain placid with a "poker face" was part of the gambler's strategy. Moreover, he had to keep tight control of his cards so that he wouldn't reveal them to any of the other players. It was different in craps where he and the others were boisterous and shouting words of encouragement or dejection with each roll of the dice. In throwing dice, there was an outlet for releasing his tensions, shouting and laughing raucously. Poker with the professional gamblers was serious business. When Joe played with his sister and other relatives, he was much more relaxed. He loved to show friends and relatives that he was a skillful bluffer. A bluffer is one who, by different mannerisms and enthusiastic raising of the pot as games progress, makes people think he has a better hand than he actually has. A good bluffer will best an opponent who has a better hand.

Just as in dice, there are several ways to cheat in poker. The professional gambler may capitalize on chance when playing a naive player who is unaware of the odds. A gambler may alter the odds by slipping new cards in his hand and discarding others when the players are not looking carefully. The most common way to change the odds in poker is bluffing. The player who bluffs convinces others that he has a better hand than he does. I remember watching Joe in a game of poker. His hand consisted of a pair of eights. He leaned over and whispered to me, "Watch this!" Joe called and raised the pot by twice the amount. Two players dropped (folded) immediately. One player called and raised the ante slightly, and another did the same. Joe doubled the ante again, and another player dropped out. The last player folded after Joe doubled the ante still another time. During this betting, Joe was poker-faced, not saying a word. When the game was over, Joe took the pot and put his cards face down so the other players didn't know whether he was bluffing or not. Joe put a show on for me, and it worked. After the game he bubbled with pleasure, knowing he had outsmarted the other gamblers.

Joe was careful to avoid repetitious patterns. He didn't bluff every game. Some games he'd lose, showing he only had a pair. The object was to keep the other players guessing. If only Joe had avoided repetition the night of his murder! Every Sunday evening he would go home to watch an FBI story with Elliot Ness and the army of bad guys, Al Capone, Scar Faced Nelson, and so forth. His murderers knew he'd be home to watch another FBI story. If he hadn't come at that time, it's conceivable that they would have left his house before he arrived.

Joe taught me some of the basic rules of poker. However, he didn't play with me. He admonished me not to play because it was too easy to lose. Poker to him was a game of strategy and calculation. Although probabilities were involved, the strategies of risk taking and bluffing appeared to be dominant. As Kenny Rogers sang in "The Gambler," you've got to know "when to hold 'em and when to fold 'em." One has to know whether he's being bluffed and whether his hand is sufficient to win. In contrast, playing dice is "a crap shoot." You usually don't know whether you will win. It's more primitive. The game is over with a roll of the dice.

One advantage Joe had in playing any card game was his prodigious memory. He instantly memorized all the cards that were displayed, observing who had what. If a game was based on using one deck of fifty-two cards, or two decks of one hundred and four cards, etc., the odds would change with each hand dealt. For example, if there are four Aces in a deck of fifty-two cards, and three were observed in the last hand, Joe would know that the chances of getting an Ace were altered. Phenomenally, he would be able to cite these conditional probabilities intuitively. This would increase his knowledge of possible hands immensely. Of course, there were other professional gamblers that had similar skills. I knew of no one who could compete with him in terms of memorizing the cards that were played. He was regarded as one hell of a poker player, and he took great pride in that. He liked to play with my sister for fun, being relaxed, and playing with someone who loved him unconditionally.

# LAKE TAHOE

Lake Tahoe is a recreational area in the Sierra-Nevada Mountains. The Lake has crystal-clear, blue water which is cold all year round. It's about 100 miles from Sacramento. In the summer it's an ideal vacation spot with many places to camp, hike, ride horses and swim. It's at a high elevation, and the aroma in the air is clear and crisp. To arrive there in the winter one needs to have chains on automobile tires; for it is covered with ice and snow. Many people spend weekends there to gamble. Gambling was legal in Nevada, but not in California. One casino, the Cal-Neva Lodge, was partly in California and partly in Nevada. Those in the lodge on the California side walked to the Nevada side to gamble. There were also a good number of people who went to Lake Tahoe to watch the stars from Hollywood perform in the casinos, Cal-Neva, Harrah's, etc. My sister had a cabin in Donner Pass, which is on the way to Lake Tahoe and is the place where the Donner party of history engaged in cannibalism to survive the trek over the mountains. My sister and her family loved the mountains, especially in the summer. Winters were severe. The cabin was often buried under twenty feet of snow. Upkeep was costly, so my sister sold the cabin after several years.

Joe and his wife, Phil and her husband Aubrey, and other couples didn't drive to Lake Tahoe on Friday nights to look only at the scenery and breathe in the Alpine air. They also went to gamble, eat and watch the shows. Phil would play Blackjack and the slot machines, and Joe played Craps and Blackjack. The atmosphere in the casino was one of a steady hum, bells and buzzers sounding off about jackpot winners, glasses of beer, wine, and liquor tinkling, and the mechanical pulling of the one-armed bandits, the slot machines.

I was awe-struck when I first watched people playing the slot machines. They hovered over the machines in a semi-hypnotic trance, for hours at a time. They were compelled to pull that handle and hope for a jackpot, often settling for three oranges for twenty coins and other smaller denominations such as one cherry for two coins, eventually losing their money. At that time in the 1950's the cheapest slot machine was one nickel, five cents. That's what I played when I went with a friend for a weekend. I quickly got sucked into the habit of pulling the lever. It was compelling, and I found myself behaving strangely like the people I watched. I became possessive of the machine and didn't like it if people played the machine next to mine. If there were to be a jackpot, I wanted it to be mine. Nevertheless, I stuck with Joe's warning not to gamble, and only played for a few dollars.

Joe was a high roller. He was in that exclusive set of gamblers for whom casinos provided free rooms, suites, food, and liquor. Of course, high rollers had to spend a large amount of money gambling. As a high roller, Joe and his entourage would have the best accommodations and were wined and dined at the casino's expense. My sister and others would gamble but not with the same fervor and intensity as Joe. If gambling went well, Joe was happy.

I've only been to Lake Tahoe's casinos four or five times; hence my knowledge is quite limited. It is no secret, however, that many of the gamblers became destitute. Moreover, young women often went to Nevada to seek a quick divorce, much as my mother did in Reno, Nevada, when Joe was three. Divorcees often worked in the casinos as barmaids, croupiers, and Blackjack dealers. Others, down and out, turned tricks for money. Johns were available twenty-four hours a day, while sleepless gamblers obsessively pursued their dreams of riches or recovery from huge losses.

Joe was a man of action, a bookie, a gambler. He was a bon vivant in his intense dedication to life and the good times that accrued to high rollers in casinos at Lake Tahoe, Las Vegas, Atlantic City and elsewhere. His card game at Lake Tahoe was Blackjack. Joe knew a number of strategies for winning at Blackjack very well. He had an additional advantage. He could memorize which cards had been played, thereby increasing his knowledge about which strategies to employ. Essentially when Joe played he was a card counter; and, when only one deck was used, Joe would usually win. He won thousands of dollars at Blackjack. Later on in time I read about card counters and how they were banned from playing at casinos. Remarkably, Joe was a card counter before the term became popularized. The solution that casinos came up with was to play more than one deck at a time. This makes the procedure of memorizing cards much more difficult, decreasing the advantage of the card counter. Blackjack and Craps are games in which the odds for a player to beat the house are relatively even. Joe was calm in the casino when he was winning but became agitated when losing. Craps, his compulsion, depended more on sheer luck than skill. Even at the casino, crap games instilled in the players an excitement. Players shouted as if somehow the noise would psychokinetically influence the dice. What was exciting for players who bet either for or against the house was when the person rolling the dice was on a streak, "on a roll." Then the atmosphere resembled the din of players' voices in the back alleys where a floating crap game was occurring. When Joe lost big time, he became violently angry, not wanting to talk to anybody. He would shout and swear and sometimes turn over tables in the casino. He hated to lose, becoming obnoxious and unpleasant. Our kind sister said with affection in her voice, "He was crazy; he had a temper." His wives probably hated it when he lost, preferring the victory toast of "The drinks are on me." Joe loved his celebrity status as a high roller, and he enjoyed treating his friends and relatives to a good time at Lake Tahoe.

# HORSE RACES

Joe's profession was bookmaking. He took bets from his clientele on horse races. Probably he learned some of the basic ingredients from Butch Nisetich, Sacramento's famed gambler, at the Alhambra Bowling Alley. He learned the nitty gritty of his craft by his intelligence, intuition and experience. Since it was an illegal activity, he had to keep on moving his place of business so he wouldn't be detected by the police. His office floated, as in floating craps. He worked in bars on J street, Broadway near the Tower Drugs, his home, and in other places. Joe wrote his transactions on slips of paper so no one except he could decipher the contents. Leonardo da Vinci wrote upside down and reversed the writing so it could only be deciphered in a mirror. In that way only he could decipher his new knowledge on art, anatomy, engineering, and aviation. In the spirit of Da Vinci, Joe developed a number code which only he was able to decode. He recorded who was betting for how much on which horse and which race with what odds. Bets became very complicated, but Joe was able to handle them. The bookie has to know many things about horse racing. For example, he has to know the history of the horse that's running. Past performance is fairly predictive, but it's not enough. One has to know about the jockey, the condition of the track where the horse is running, the weather, e.g., whether the horse races well in the mud, odds that are set in the racing form, the other horses running and so forth. Joe quickly analyzed all the information provided on racing forms, and he also utilized any information he could get from horse owners, jockeys, grooms, etc. If everyone who bet against a bookie won, the bookie would soon be out of business. Likewise, if all of those insured could make a claim on an insurance policy, the insurance company would go bankrupt. Making money in insurance is based on the same premise as in bookmaking. The insurer or the bookmaker has to capitalize on chance. The odds have to be in their favor. When one's insurance rates are increased after an accident, the insurer is simply changing the odds.

Joe began his practice of bookmaking while he was completing his apprenticeship as a cake decorator at the Channel Pie Bakery. When he was in his 30s in the 1960s he progressed to the point where he was the premier bookie in Sacramento and, perhaps, Northern California. Joe and his friends would travel from race track to race track to bet on horses as well as increase their knowledge about the racing system.

Joe and his buddies drove in his latest Cadillac convertible, stopping to eat in the finest restaurants throughout California. Returning to Sacramento from a one or two day trip, Joe often stopped at the Nut Tree, a restaurant between Vacaville and Sacramento. He would buy toys for his children and eat the famous Nut Tree bread and sandwiches. Although Joe loved to eat in expensive, fancy restaurants in San Francisco and environs, his idea of gourmet food continued to be a hunk of pepperoni, a jar of hot green peppers, and a loaf of French or Italian bread.

There were a lot of pressures on a bookie, especially when Joe was active. In the 50s and 60s there wasn't the rapid communication system that we have now. Many who placed bets with Joe tried to cheat, and he had to be wary, "on his toes." For example, one client placed a bet with Joe on a horse in a race from Chicago and claimed he won. The problem was that the race was over when the client bet. Joe discovered this by several phone calls and immediately scratched that person as a customer.

Horse races are exciting. The bell rings, and they're off on a quick tour of the track. Those who bet on horses look for cues that might help. They might look at the horse's demeanor before the race. If the horse is overactive, agitated and tense, some would interpret that as the horse is anxious to run and should do well. Others might think the horse is drugged, frightened, or sick. Most of us amateurs think of things that might bring luck. We bet on special names, numbers, races, and so forth. That kind of information doesn't change the odds on winning. Nevertheless, it helps us to believe we have some control over the outcome of a particular race. Amateurs probably bet in relation to some aspect of their personalities.

My brother Tommy, Joe, Phil and Aub went to the California State Fair every year to bet on horses at the track. I sometimes went to watch the horses, but I didn't bet. The only times I bet were with my children two or three times in a lifetime. I was still trying to follow Joe's admonitions about gambling. The races lasted for one to two weeks at the State Fair. It was vacation time for Tommy, Phil, and Aub. They bet recreationally and typically over a week's span won or lost about $100.

I remembered a person who got a tip from one who was grooming horses. He ran about a half mile to be able to place his bet before the race started. He got there too late. Fortunately or unfortunately, depending upon one's view of life, the horse won. The unrequited gambler turned pale, thinking of how it might have been if only he were faster. Tears appeared in his eyes and he cried out in a losing roar of despair, "Shit, I could've won!"

Joe was the cool professional at those races. He had a special place to park his Cadillac, near the grandstand. Aub, Phil's husband, said he felt like a celebrity when he parked Joe's car and then went to bet. Nearby in a Pavilion there were scrumptious lunches for big shot executives, businessmen, and state officials. Joe and those with him ate with the elite, a kind of junior high roller's club at the State Fair.

Joe was very careful when he bet. Approximately one year before his death, he was followed by internal revenue agents, people looking for tips on betting, and Willie the Weasel who had ties with the Mafia. To divert his followers, Joe would give a large sum of money to either Tommy or Aub to bet upstairs and a smaller sum of money to the other to bet downstairs. Joe's real bet could have been placed with either Aubrey or Tommy. They were his runners. Joe would place a modest bet himself at a different window.

Aub recounted the story that he went to one window to collect his winnings (for Joe), and he received $4,000. Behind him was the State Director of the Water Resources. Aub was also a state employee, and his job was to repair calculators. A few races later, the Director of Water Resources again saw Aub collect another $2,000. At work the following Monday, Aub noticed the Director, making inquiries about him, thinking that Aub was a professional gambler. Aub loved Joe, and he felt good when he received some of the status attributed to him. In a sense, Joe was a celebrity.

Joe had a ranch with a lot of acreage. He bought several horses so he and friends could ride them. They were race horses. After he bought them, he realized it would take several weeks before they would calm down. They ran in races, and they were drugged. At that time, the laws against doping horses were either not in effect or not strictly enforced.

The horse is a beautiful, graceful animal when it is healthy and treated well. Probably, the most intriguing horses are those that are wild, the legendary wild mustangs. It is depressing, however, to see a broken-down nag, who tried against his will to run but was unsuccessful. It's analogous to the punch-drunk fighter who has nothing left to do in life after having been beaten over and over. Joe's children, step children, nephews, and nieces enjoyed riding the horses. Joe, friendly with horse owners as well as jockeys, sometimes invited jockeys to come to dinner at his ranch and relax by playing pool or riding the horses to the American River.

There was one dinner in which Joe and his relatives, a jockey, and an owner of a car dealership were in attendance. The jockey, Jackie Robinson (not the famous baseball player), said he was going to ride *Bunny Girl* in an upcoming race. He emphatically announced he was going to win. The car dealer named Sacco bet $50 on the horse to win. Bunny Girl was a long shot. The horse won, paying $49.80 for every dollar wagered; so Sacco won $2,490 by coming to dinner at Joe's ranch.

There is a story that Willie the Weasel went to Joe's restaurant, The Buggy Whip, and told Joe he represented the Mafia. He wanted a part of Joe's action (i.e., his book making customers). Joe literally threw him out of the restaurant, saying he wasn't afraid of him or the Mafia.

Willie, of course, could have been lying. He might have wanted the action for himself. Years after Joe's death, Willie became an informer, ratting on his presumed allies in the Mafia. Moreover, he told people in Sacramento that he beat up Joe and that, "Joe was nothing." The police did question him about Joe's murder, but there was no evidence that Willie the Weasel was involved. He wrote a book about his work with the Mafia, and he mentioned Joe Torchia, describing him as a West coast gambler who thought he was bigger than he was. It sounded like "sour grapes," but there is no way of knowing what really happened.

The horse races still take place every year. There continue to be stories of the races, touts, bookies, and the agony and ecstasy of customers winning and losing. Probably agents of the Internal Revenue Service and small-time mobsters follow and even stalk some of the gamblers. Joe isn't on the gambling scene now, but his spirit lives in the stories that people tell about him. They light up, smiling, recalling those days when he was at the peak of his profession. And, when placing bets at the State Fair, many conjure up his image and think of the days when gambling was at its height in Sacramento.

# THE DOWNSIDE OF BOOKMAKING

The life of a bookie has its glamour, particularly when there is a large clientele that gets paid when winning and pays when losing. The income can be very good, and many activities can be fun. In addition, there is an element of power for those bookies who are successful, allowing access to night clubs, bars, restaurants and other forms of entertainment. However, there is a downside to bookmaking.

Bookies need to pay off winners, and they need to have enough money to do so. The clientele range from the upper classes to the down-trodden; and if they are not paid, they can try to beat up the bookie or have others do it. It's also possible that dissatisfied customers can inform the police. In contrast, the bookie has to be able to collect from his customers. If the clients don't pay on time, the bookie has the problem of collecting payments. All of this assumes that the bookie has an accurate account of bets and bettors. Joe always paid off on time. He had amassed a reserve of cash over and beyond the cash placed on debts. The reserve was necessary in case there were a large number of winners on a given day of betting. The act of responsibly paying on time enhanced Joe's reputation as reliable, one whose word could be trusted. As his reputation for reliability increased, there were fewer cheaters and fewer customers who would avoid paying if they lost. Joe's memory and his system of keeping his own notes on customer's bets enabled him to be very accurate. But there were some who wouldn't pay up right away. Joe knew where they were, and he'd arrange to meet them in a bar. I went with him a couple of times when he was collecting payments at a bar on J Street. Joe first reminded them they owed money. Then, he asked why no payments were made. He was able to read customers well. He could tell if they were lying or not. When Joe felt one was telling the truth about having to take care of his family, he would defer payments. If the person had no excuse or was lying, Joe would give him a warning. I don't know what he said, but most of the customers paid up right away. I presume he threatened them in some way, but I never knew. I never saw Joe use his fists and beat people up; however, I believe he was capable of exerting physical punishment. Some people hire other people to do the dirty work, i.e., to collect payments. As in organized crime, these enforcers do nothing but bully people and "beat the shit out of them if they don't pay up." I never saw these enforcers, but I clearly understood that they were the dregs of humanity. They were two-bit thugs who were psychopathic, enhancing their inflated images of themselves, irrespective of whether they beat up teenagers or old men. They were like the hit men in the Mafia. They worked in cities like Brooklyn, Chicago, and Boston, and they used their baseball bats for intimidating people. I don't believe Joe used enforcers. I heard him say he had to collect payments himself. However, it is possible that some of his friends collected for him as his action increased.

If the Internal Revenue Service suspects one of gambling, making large sums of money, and not filing income tax returns, it assigns agents to keep an eye on the suspected gambler. When agents followed Joe at the race track, they were trying to gather evidence they could use to prosecute him for illegal activities. The police will also try to prosecute a gambler if they have a sufficient amount of evidence that could be used in court. Often police receive tips about gamblers from anonymous persons, usually those who are angry at the gambler for events in their personal lives or disgruntled bettors. When Joe was in his 20s he was arrested in his home. The police received a tip, and they seized his notes. At that time he wrote names and amounts of bets on slips of paper. Joe got a good lawyer who argued that the police didn't have a search warrant, so the evidence was inadmissible. Joe wasn't prosecuted. He was arrested again shortly thereafter. The police found no slips of paper, and they had to release Joe. Undoubtedly that led Joe to devise a number system for keeping track of bets that nobody but he could decode.

These experiences led Joe to lament the fact that he didn't receive more education. He thought he would have made a good lawyer. He knew thoroughly the laws that might affect him in his chosen profession. Curiously, my mother had similar experiences in a legal enterprise. She bought houses, renovating and renting them. She rented rooms and apartments. Both my mother and Joe had the necessary skills to be lawyers. They had excellent memories, were intelligent, and had "street smarts." However, they simply did not have the education.

The life of a lawyer working in a firm that makes a lot of money was Joe's idea of a life he could have had. In his work as a bookie he had to be alert, watching his clientele carefully and paying attention to strange people who might be following him. Obviously, the biggest downside of being a bookie is that it's dangerous. One might end up in prison. One might lose a lot of money. One might even be murdered.

# THE BUGGY WHIP

Americans wishing to change jobs often think of owning a restaurant, a farm, or some other small business. We romanticize the idea of being in charge and doing what we consider the good things in life. The less we know about the running of business the more romantic our thoughts become. In the restaurant world, we think of serving the best of foods, wines, and liquors. It's only when we look at restaurants more closely do we realize it takes long hours of hard work each day to operate one. Worries about the food supplies, the cooking, whether or not people will order the food on hand, the desires of customers, attracting customers, obtaining a liquor license, keeping the accounts and payrolls in order, and so forth. One even has to watch the employees to ensure that they're not eating into whatever profits are made.

In 1959 Joe became a restaurateur. As he progressed in this new career, he spent more time on managing the restaurant and a little less time in traveling to different places to gamble. Owning a restaurant was another way for Joe to make money. Primarily it was a vehicle for his integration into white collar society, the business world. His activities became legitimate.

The first year of the restaurant business was hectic for Joe. He became a partner with several other owners. Very organized and hard working with a genius for management, he acted intuitively as if he had experience beyond the M.B.A. The owners argued over a name for the restaurant until Joe came up with the name of "The Buggy Whip." A buggy whip is the whip that jockeys use on horses in harness races. The jockey sits in the buggy, chariot, or cart that is pulled by the horse.

Most of the partners appeared to be incompetent. They weren't that interested in working to make money, and they weren't trying hard to increase the numbers of patrons. Within a year's time, Joe bought out most of the other partners. In that way with the blessing of another partner he could be more aggressive in running the restaurant. Joe met his wife-to-be Jeanne in the restaurant bar. He soon moved in with her, asking her to straighten out the accounts which were in total disarray. Jeanne didn't want to do it; so, as usual in a crisis, he turned to our sister Phil. He asked her to keep the books, accounts, ledgers, etc., and he paid her $25.00 a week. In a sense, he came to her for help and then used her by paying a very low wage for straightening up the books and keeping track of the accounts. She did this until his death in 1970. To increase the patronage Joe came up with a gimmick. For $5 he offered a special steak dinner with champagne for two. He made deals with a butcher and the owner of a liquor store to get steaks and champagne at reduced prices. Huge crowds of people came to the restaurant, which seated 70-100. They were looking for a bargain. They got what they wanted but had to wait for up to an hour to be served. Naturally, they ordered drinks at the bar. Profits soared as a result of the increased expenditures on liquor. The restaurant was in a safe place that was accessible in the eastern part of Sacramento. Word quickly got around, and Joe's first and only venture in the restaurant business was successful.

I once attended a meeting that Joe had at his ranch with other restaurateurs. Being naive about protection, control of products, and other shady activities of the business world, I was utterly amazed to hear those businessmen decide who would be the chief distributor of various staples such as cooking oil, sugar, and so forth. Joe was in charge of lard, setting the prices for a number of restaurants.

Joe employed Phil, Aub, and their son Jimmy as well as Tommy and some other family members to work in the restaurant. With the exception of Phil who did the accounts and Tommy who took receipts and cash to Phil for her accounting, the work they did was focused on setting up tables and cleaning the restaurant. So far as I know all of the family was completely trustworthy. This was not the case with other employees. Waiters often dipped in the till (the cash register) and the bartenders, who were the chief offenders, stole money from customers. Joe had an ingenious method for checking on the bartenders. First he counted the number of bottles of wine and liquor that were at hand.

After business at the end of a day, Aub, Tommy and Jimmy counted the remaining bottles. Subtracting them from the original numbers and types of wines and liquors, Joe then calculated the value of the drinks that could have been made. If the cash for the sales on a particular day was less than the estimated value of drinks, it was clear to Joe that the bartender was siphoning money from the till. Then Joe would confront the bartender, verify the accuracy of his method, and fire him. My brother Joe may not have had any training in measurement and the scientific method as promulgated by the great Galileo, but he sure knew how to apply scientific thinking to catching cheats in gambling as well as in his restaurant.

There were some amusing incidents in the restaurant. Bartenders were not supposed to drink. A group of society women came to the restaurant, and they began drinking. They drank until they were soused. The bartender, enamored of the idea of drinking with so many good looking women, joined them. They were all plastered in an orgy of drinking. Joe, of course, fired that bartender.

Joe got a call one day from the coach of a football team in the state of Washington. The Washington team was to play Sacramento State's football team. The coach told Joe he heard the food in the restaurant was good, and he asked if Joe could feed his team at 5:00 p.m. before most of the regular customers came in. Joe thought maybe fifteen-twenty guys would be coming to the restaurant. He forgot that teams often traveled with fifty players. They came, and they kept coming—the football team, the coaches, the cheerleaders, and university officials. Joe was close to panic, but kept his cool, calling for family and friends to come immediately to help out. Big, burly football players ate with huge appetites. Some players ate three steak dinners apiece. It was great business, but the number was unexpected. Joe did adapt and worked feverishly through the storm of the visiting football team. There was a lot of sweat on everyone working that night. Afterwards, they laughed, reminiscing about it years later.

Since Joe was a gambler, it was inevitable that he would integrate gambling with his new profession. The restaurant was opened for lunch every day except Christmas and New Year's Day at 11:30 a.m. And on each Saturday, prior to opening for the public, Joe hosted card games and breakfast from 6:30 a.m. to 9:00 a.m. Businessmen, gamblers, and professional men came to eat crabmeat and eggs and other delights while they gambled. Those times were pure joy for him. He was the host. Friends ate at his restaurant, and they all gambled. They made a lot of noise and had a great time. They usually argued about different aspects of the games they played. Tempers flared, but they cooled down before the game ended. It was as if it were group therapy with the objective of venting pent-up frustrations by means of the card games.

There were others who tried to cheat when the restaurant was open for business. These were the white collar criminals, radio and TV personalities, and other big time operators. They would sign for their bills and charge it to their companies, but they weren't authorized to do so. My sister detected this in her bookkeeping. The blue collar criminals were at it also. Some of the waiters found ways to steal food; for example, a waiter would get a big hunk of meat, wrap it up carefully, and put it in a garbage can outside. When he finished work, he'd slip it out of the garbage can and take it home.

Joe always brought meats and other kinds of food to my sister's house. The food was shared with all the other relatives. So, in addition to paying family members modest sums of money, Joe also paid them in kind with the best foods available. His restaurant was first class, and Joe had deals going with many of the food suppliers.

Joe's restaurant became a market place for vendors from as far as Los Angeles. During the Saturday morning card games, one person would come in with men's and women's suits, shoes, fur coats and other items. The highest quality of merchandise was sold at discounts ranging from 25 to 75 percent. Aub remembered Joe buying a $400 suit for him at $100. Diamonds and other jewelry were also offered for sale.

More than likely, the wares of those merchants from other cities were "hot," i.e., they were stolen. The market place served as a place for customers to act as "fences," serving those who bought stolen property. No one asked whether or not the items were stolen. They usually bought those things they liked. I remember the day when Joe had several fur coats, distributing them to his female relatives. Perhaps, he bought them at the restaurant at his Saturday morning market place. In the last five years of his life, Joe continued to prosper in the restaurant business. Nevertheless, every Saturday he played cards; and every Sunday he went to a real market place, a produce market, playing dice behind it.

Joe thought of expanding his restaurant business. He had an offer to set up a new restaurant in another part of town, and he was considering it just before his death. It's extremely difficult to be successful in the restaurant business. I've noticed many restaurants come and go. They represented the ideas of people who had different tastes in food. What is amazing is that Joe was inordinately successful. He worked hard, but he also took risks. Full of charm, he was able to persuade one and all to come to his restaurant. The conversation, food and drink were *par excellence*. It was a place where people gossiped and "hung out" at night in the bar. Joe met a host of other women there. Joe did not become a lawyer who passed the bar. However, he was a charming, complicated, and intelligent man who spent a great deal of time at his "bar." He told stories. He made jokes. He bought drinks for people. Joe got his hands dirty and learned all aspects of the restaurant business, including how to handle cheaters. Evidently many of the skills he developed in judging and playing with people in games of chance were transferable to the restaurant business. When I see a harness race on television, and I watch the jockey whipping his horse, I think of The Buggy Whip. It became an institution, and people in Sacramento talked about it a great deal. Joe's charisma continued to pervade those areas in which he worked. He could influence and move people. He knew when to take a chance, and he sensed the mood of people around him. He knew when to "hold 'em," whether they were cards or napkins in The Buggy Whip. Joe the gambler became a restaurateur.

# *Retirement Dreams*

# RETIREMENT

My brother Joe retired from the field of cake decorating at the age of twenty-one. He was an official member of the Baker's Union, and he completed all of his apprenticeship requirements. He had no pension, and he chose another line of work which capitalized on games of chance: gambling and bookmaking. Twenty years later, at the time of his death, Joe contemplated retirement again. He was managing his restaurant, bookmaking, and gambling. In other words, he was self-employed and working in two different professions: one was legitimate, and the other was illegal. Joe was of two minds. On the one hand, he was considering an offer to expand the restaurant business, opening another one, and retiring from bookmaking. On the other hand, he bought property on the island of Maui, and he was considering possible retirement as a change of scenery, a change of venue. I doubt that Joe would have sought rest and recreation only. At forty-one he was still an energetic, vibrant man. Undoubtedly, he would have found a way to gamble. More than likely, he would have entered into new schemes, business, or otherwise, to make more money.

My brother Joe was forced into retirement from all activities. His life was ended in shots to the head. He lived fast and died young. Unlike the fiction character Nick Romano who lived fast, died young, and had a good-looking corpse, Joe's corpse was brutal. His body was so mutilated that the coffin was closed during the entire proceedings at the funeral.

Often when one is retired we think of her/his impact on others and what that person learned in her/his lifetime.

In Joe's youth he amazed people with his energy and his desire to make money in whatever ways were possible. He sold newspapers. He shined shoes. He sold cushions at the automobile races. He set pins at the Alhambra Bowling Alley. He lagged coins. He made bets. Joe had outstanding hand-eye coordination, and he developed skills in shooting baskets, shooting pool, playing ping pong, putting golf balls, and bowling strikes. With supreme confidence, Joe bet on himself in those games, and he won over ninety percent of the time. He attracted people to him, and he was befriended by the biggest gamblers in Sacramento. They taught him about odds, poker, dice, and the horse races. Joe could instantly calculate odds at winning, losing, and various combinations thereof for all of the games of chance he encountered. Joe was a "ladies' man." He charmed young and old women alike. He was the kid who had his pick of the girls.

Joe learned how to read the emotions of men in the Merchant Marine. He knew when men were weak. He knew which ones were "born suckers," and he knew who the cheaters were. Joe learned about the sea and how he could bring tough seamen to their knees in a crap game. He learned how to sell cake for more than it was worth. Not only did he learn how to capitalize on the odds, but he also learned how to capitalize on people's emotions when they were gambling.

During his youth, Joe's relationship with our mother was tenuous. Joe learned how to suppress his feelings, to not publicly show his hurt. He was a teenager when our mother kicked him out of her house. Joe lived with Phil and Aub, and he learned that they cared about him in a very special way.

Joe entered his manhood at twenty-one, a retired cake decorator, a person who knew how to book the horses and how to engage customers to make wagers. He married and showed that he had a deep affection for children whether or not they were his. Joe continued to charm women, but he had difficulty in sustaining an intimate relationship. He trusted his sister, but not his wives. His relationship with our mother was ambivalent. Her love was not constant. It was conditional, depending on her state of mind. Her attitude toward Joe softened when he paid all of her expenses for a trip to her native Italy. The last four years of her life she mellowed considerably. She was blind and lived in the room my sister had built for Joe.

Our mother was entombed in a vault in the Mausoleum at St. Mary's Cemetery. Joe had a vault reserved for him near hers. Soon after her death, Joe went into the restaurant business. It was as if he were honoring our mother's pleas for him to engage in legitimate work. Cake decorating was legitimate as was the restaurant business.

Joe perfected his skills in gambling, bookmaking, and the restaurant business. He knew how to make deals, and how to negotiate that which was most favorable for him. He knew how to bluff at poker. He could detect cheaters at cards and in business. He could organize people, but he couldn't prevent them from cheating whenever they could. Joe was tough, and he used his fists if verbal persuasion didn't work. Yet, he was soft-hearted with children and with adults who had a hard time making ends meet. To those who were young, loyal, and in hard times, Joe was a philanthropist; but he downplayed his philanthropic activities.

Joe learned how to please customers at his restaurant. They ate and drank well at reasonable prices. He was generous to all of his family, helping them financially and feeding them. He took over our mother's role. Bringing tons of quality food to the family, Joe too said, "Mangia! Mangia!" (Eat! Eat!).

# RESTING

My brother Joe lived a fast, eventful life. He was loved, and he loved. He was full of life. He overcame any fears he had by taking action. Joe believed he was capable of accomplishing anything by his strong will, enormous energy, and his many talents.

Joe became a legend before his forced retirement. People smiled when they talked about him, recalling extraordinary gambling feats and humorous stories about how he bested opponents in his professions.

Joe considered retiring in the Hawaiian Islands. He was a little tired of the many conflicting situations he had to manage. In a sense, he was thinking about the beauty and the comforts of the sea. Our mother loved the sea and unlike many immigrants she spoke fondly of her voyage from Italy to the United States of America. Joe too loved the sea. He also loved our mother. He now rests in a vault at St. Mary's cemetery near her. Jack London described the plight of his character Martin Eden by quoting from a poem of Keats. This excerpt could also be used to describe my brother Joe's return to his mother,

> "...from too much love of living,
> and fear and hope set free,
> we give brief Thanksgiving
> to whatever Gods may be,
> that no man lives forever,
> that dead men rise up never,
> and even the weariest river
> winds somewhere safe to sea."

# Epilogue

Joe's story is that of a man who loved gambling. He made and spent a great deal of money in his lifetime. A son of Italian immigrants, he showed that he could rise in his socioeconomic class by hard work, wit, and intelligence. He was one of Sacramento's premier gamblers. Murdered at the age of forty-one, he made his mark in the illegal world of bookmaking and gambling, as well as in the legal world of the restaurant business. He was a human being who lived in a world of action. His own actions probably resulted in his murder, which to this day is unsolved.

In remembering him today we each think of him from our own perspective. My brother Tommy, a baseball player in the Sports Hall of Fame in Sacramento, California, recalls Joe's generosity to his family and children; and he is amazed at the raw athletic talent that Joe displayed in basketball, billiards, golf, ping pong, etc.

Phil excels in accounting and business. She thought of Joe as a shrewd businessman who knew how to make money. He excelled at negotiation, making a deal that would favor him. She recently realized that Joe didn't pay her as much as he could have for keeping the accounting records of his restaurant. Yet, she regards him with love and misses the charisma and charm that exuded from his very being.

Phil's husband Aubrey is quite a raconteur. He loves to tell stories about the character of Joe, the legend who still lives. Aubrey said, "I could talk about Joe for hours and hours. He really was quite a character."

I, a Dean and college professor, marveled at Joe's intelligence. He calculated in his head probabilities for the gambling events in which he was engaged. Joe remembered everything, and he used his store of information to his advantage. He was a real life character straight out of fiction.

We miss him.

0-595-26448-4

Made in the USA
Lexington, KY
12 July 2012